Popular Library

TX
823
.M68
1981

Morton, Nancy Alice.

Picnics with pizzazz

DATE			

Picnics with Pizzazz

Picnics with Pizzazz

Nancy Alice Morton

Illustrations by Sandy Roush

Contemporary Books, Inc.
Chicago

Library of Congress Cataloging in Publication Data

Morton, Nancy Alice.
   Picnics with pizzazz.

   Includes index.
   1. Outdoor cookery.   2. Picnicking.   3. Menus.
I. Title.
TX823.M68   1981   642'.3   80-70642
ISBN 0-8092-5922-2 (pbk.)   AACR2

Copyright © 1981 by Nancy Alice Morton
All rights reserved
Published by Contemporary Books, Inc.
180 North Michigan Avenue, Chicago, Illinois 60601
Manufactured in the United States of America
Library of Congress Catalog Card Number: 80-70642
International Standard Book Number: 0-8092-5922-2

Published simultaneously in Canada by
Beaverbooks, Ltd.
150 Lesmill Road
Don Mills, Ontario M3B 2T5
Canada

To ELLA
for whom cooking was a picnic
and pizzazz a way of life.

Contents

Introduction: Picnic Fundamentals

Approach each picnic as though you were planning a party and you will be well on the way to a picnic with pizzazz. Add superb food presented with flair and you have the makings of a most delightful excursion.

There's plenty of precedent for this enthusiastic combination of fun, fine food, and drama. The word *pique-nique* was coined by the French to designate a particular form of entertainment. And, for a period later in its history, this group activity regularly included amateur theatricals as well as a meal. All participants were expected to contribute either talent or food.

If the theatricals were amateur, however, the food was not, for these excursions were fashionable as well as popular. The short jaunts to a charming country location were social events. Today's excursions can still incorporate any or all of the elements of style or theater that characterized the picnic's beginnings.

Each chapter in this book approaches these happy outings from a slightly different angle. For example, menus identified as Eclectic Excursions plan the foods around side trips to a variety of destinations. When style piques a picnic sense, the Posh Little Suppers in Chapter 2 suggest the kind of meals that turn eating outdoors into dining alfresco.

Faraway places also make good picnic themes. Even if the participants travel only a few miles from home, the menus with International Accents in Chapter 3 become passports to world-wide excursions in good eating.

Birthdays and family get-togethers provide more marvelous opportunities for celebrating with a picnic. Occasional Outings, Chapter 4, rate a place on this summer's calendar right now.

Not all excursions occupy a full evening or a whole day. Those into the business world break only briefly right at noon. Most people just have lunch. The collection of Midday Repasts in Chapter 5 sees the possibilities differently. They reason that alone or with colleagues, there's nothing like a gourmet bite to eat outdoors in the noonday sun—or shade.

The Earl of Sandwich lived during the time when *pique-niques* were developing in France and on the Continent. Whether this notable gamester took one of his creations on a picnic or not, succeeding generations have made up for his oversight. The final chapter carries on the tradition with some enticing combinations of Bread and "with it."

Once you have decided on the menu for a particular excursion, the time comes to zero in on the details that make it work. Picnic pointers appear at strategic points in the book, but here is an overview of the considerations that will make things go smoothly.

THE EQUIPMENT NEEDED TO BRING IT OFF

Taking the picnic show on the road presents special problems of logistics if hot foods are to arrive hot and cold foods are to stay thoroughly chilled. Recipes throughout the book are good troupers, but they need help from packing techniques that assure the food will look and taste its best when presented. Good management behind the scenes and en route also includes proper handling from a food safety standpoint.

For all that picnic baskets or hampers conjure up romantic images of picnicking, baskets do very little to protect the food. In practice, almost nothing in the food line except breads, cookies, and crackers leaves the kitchen unless it is boiling hot or well chilled and stowed in the appropriate containers to keep it that way.

Versatile insulated chests and vacuum jugs take most of the worry out of keeping picnic food safe as well as holding the food at the right serving temperature. The handy carriers range in size from something slightly larger than a lunch box to enormous coolers with a capacity of twelve gallons. In addition, there are zippered pouches and an assortment of large and small widemouth containers for hot or cold liquids.

Hot Foods

Since there is no hot equivalent to the ice cube, the layered look is the method for keeping foods warm. Wrap hot foot in several thicknesses of newspaper, then overwrap with heavy towels or such things as a car robe or child's quilt, or place in an insulated carrier. In the case of soups or hot beverages, preheat vacuum bottles or jugs by filling with boiling water and allowing them to stand a few minutes.

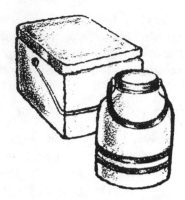

Cold Foods

Chilled foods keep their cool longer if ice or some other coolant is packed with them. You can make your own ice cubes or buy them in bulk. Or, if you don't need cubes for beverages, you can freeze water in washed milk cartons or plastic bowls with tight-fitting lids. However, frozen water in any form is bulky and wet. That is why campers and hunters use the sealed containers of refreezable gel sold in sporting goods stores. Freeze them like ice in the home freezer and pack on top of food. The gel thaws at a slower rate than ice and takes up less room in the cooler.

Dry ice can be used to maintain low temperatures, but it must be wrapped heavily and handled carefully with thick gloves. Besides the inconvenience of locating a place to buy it, the handling precautions limit its practicality for most picnics.

Vacuum bottles may be chilled by setting them in the refrigerator or packing them with ice before use. Either practice extends their cooling ability considerably.

The types of equipment available will not only influence your choice of food, but also the quality and the variety of beverages offered.

PICNIC BEVERAGES

You can classify picnic drinks by serving temperature, by presence or absence of bubbles, and by alcoholic content. Each category presents certain possibilities and problems.

In general, considerations of temperature are similar to those for food. There are vacuum bottles and jugs for hot drinks and ice chests and vacuum jugs for cold ones.

The presence of bubbles or carbonation changes the picture. Vacuum jugs cannot be used, since the pressure from the released gasses inside can weaken the seal on the jug.

Beer and Soft Drinks: Cans in six- and twelve-packs chill relatively quickly in ice. Having them at refrigerator temperature to start saves some of the ice power. Among the newest of insulated carriers are those designed specifically to accommodate these packs of cans.

Champagne and Sparkling Water: Refrigerate these before leaving home and carry to picnic in an ice chest.

Wine: Reconciling picnic temperatures and the recommended room temperature for certain wines takes some doing. Fortunately, there are a good many delicious choices among the moderately priced wines; so, leaving the fine expensive ones for more prestigious occasions is no sacrifice. In general, an ice chest for picnic wines is the best bet. Technically, most red wines don't need chilling, but on a hot day you may enjoy them more after a short while on ice. Serving wine over ice cubes is another cooling possibility. Again, already having the wine at a cool temperature keeps cubes from melting too quickly.

You might use each picnic as an opportunity to get acquainted with a wine you have read about but not sampled. Over the picnic

season not only will you be more knowledgeable about what the experts mean by sweet, dry, fruity, or crisp, but you'll also have a list of wines you would like to serve again.

Cocktails and Mixed Drinks: Wine punches such as Sangria Blanca (see index) and before-dinner drinks like Kir (see index) make refreshing picnic drinks. Also totable are the commercial mixes for mai tais, daiquiris, and bloody marys. They save you the trouble of packing the individual ingredients required to make the drinks from scratch. It is also practical to pick one drink to complement the menu or party theme and eliminate the necessity for setting up a bar at the picnic location.

Nonalcoholic Beverages: Every picnic should include at least one beverage that does not contain liquor. Some people at the party choose to skip alcohol or its extra calories. The upsurge in popularity of imported sparkling and tonic waters makes them a fashionable option to serve with a slice of lime. Other possibilities include fruit juices, soft drinks (especially diet pop), sparkling water, coffee, iced tea, and plain ice water.

Coffee is a welcome beverage after any meal and stays deliciously hot in vacuum containers. Iced tea also does well at picnics. Freeze a tray of tea ice cubes to put in the picnic jug. They won't dilute the tea as they thaw. Use plain ice cubes from the chest to put into individual tall glasses.

The planning is by no means over with the selection of food and drink. This is the time to add some razzle-dazzle.

GIVING A PICNIC PIZZAZZ

Entertaining with style and originality picks up where the menu leaves off. Inspiration may come from the food, the outing's destination, a national holiday, a world capital, or a personal whim. The tone can be quietly elegant or outrageously flamboyant. A good deal of the credit goes to the props.

A wondrous assortment of sturdy paper and plastic items, both colorful and disposable, are on the market. While the various pieces are coordinated, care should be taken that their colors and designs also are compatible with the food to be served on them.

One of the most surprising and appreciated gestures is to bring real plates and glassware. Almost more than anything, this says you care about how the food is served. Crystal stemware and sterling pieces aren't necessary. Attractive stoneware and inexpensive wine glasses show off the food to advantage and are replaceable.

Fabric tablecloths and big napkins create a grand impression, too. And, like the dishes, they need not be elaborate. Go with what you have. Besides traditional tablecloths, check the linen closet for a floral sheet. The remnant table at a fabric shop may have a piece that goes with the chosen picnic theme.

Above all—let the picnic begin!

Picnics with Pizzazz

Points of Interest

Day in the Country Lunch

Champagne Brunch

Beach Basket Special

Parade-Watcher's Box Lunch

Chichi Combination

Dinner on Deck

1

Eclectic Excursions

A favorite ingredient of most warm-weather outings or side trips is that they run right past mealtime. Where, when, and what to eat enter the planning at an early stage.

Although the avowed purpose of the jaunt may be to have a swim, take a boat ride, or simply enjoy the countryside, an imaginative choice of picnic food does more than just relieve hunger pangs. It also turns the occasion into something special.

Some picnic opportunities spring up spontaneously, and picking up bread, assorted cheeses, and a bottle of wine en route satisfies both gastronomic and esthetic requirements. More often, however, an excursion is well anticipated, with sufficient time to prepare sophisticated food in advance and assemble the necessary equipment to make serving and eating outdoors the pleasurable experience it should be.

The menus in this chapter are keyed to a variety of popular excursions. Besides suggestions for packing and carrying the foods to maintain quality and preserve safety, there are ideas for themes and utensils that carry out the meal plan.

DAY IN THE COUNTRY LUNCH

Ham and Eggplant Salad
Cream Puff Basket
Ripe Olives   Sliced Tomatoes
Pineapple with Crème de Menthe
White Wine
Iced Tea

Plan this picnic as though some quaint country inn were catering the meal. Decide that the specialty of the house is an artfully seasoned Ham and Eggplant Salad served in a Cream Puff Basket and go on from there.

Pack inexpensive stemware for the wine and something similar about the size of old-fashioned glasses for the dessert. A checkered tablecloth and pottery plates lend an appropriate rustic note.

Ham and Eggplant Salad

½ cup mayonnaise (not salad
     dressing)
1 teaspoon wine vinegar
½ small clove garlic, finely
     minced
½ teaspoon salt
¼ cup thinly sliced green onion
     with tops
¼ cup snipped parsley
1 1- to 1½-pound eggplant
1½ cups fully cooked ham cubes
     or thin strips
2 hard-cooked eggs
Romaine or leaf lettuce
Cream Puff Basket (see recipe
     below)

Blend together mayonnaise, wine vinegar, garlic, and salt. Stir in green onions and parsley. Cover and chill mixture to allow flavors to blend. Carry to picnic in insulated cooler.

Wash unpeeled eggplant and cut into ¾-inch cubes. Cook in boiling salted water only 3 minutes. Drain immediately. Toss with ham and chill in covered container. Carry to picnic in cooler.

Wash and pat dry romaine leaves or leaf lettuce. Carry to picnic in plastic bag with a crumpled paper towel in the bottom. Pack with the cold foods.

Carry hard-cooked eggs with cold foods. Peel and slice just before serving.

At serving time, toss chilled eggplant and ham with dressing. Line Cream Puff Basket with greens. Spoon in salad mixture. Garnish with sliced eggs. Cut into wedges.
Makes 6 servings

Cream Puff Basket

¼ cup butter or margarine
½ cup boiling water
½ cup all-purpose flour
¼ teaspoon salt
2 eggs

Melt butter in boiling water and bring to rolling boil. Stir in flour and salt. Stir vigorously over low heat for 1 minute. Remove from heat.

Beat in eggs all at once. Continue beating until mixture is smooth. Pat dough in bottom and up sides of an ungreased 8-inch pie pan.

Bake in 400°F. oven 30 to 40 minutes until golden brown. *Note:* Since steam is what makes basket puff, expect basket to be somewhat irregular in shape.

Slip basket out of pie pan and cool on a rack. Carry to picnic in a basket or ventilated container.
Makes 6 servings

Pineapple with Crème de Menthe

Select a plump, fresh-looking pineapple that is slightly soft to the touch and developing a yellow or reddish brown color. It should also have a pleasant fruity aroma.

To prepare: Twist the crown to remove it and cut a slice off the bottom of the fruit so it will stand upright. Grasping the standing pineapple in one hand and a sharp knife in the other, cut off the rind with downward strokes, taking as much of the eyes as possible. (Use the tip of a potato peeler to remove the remainder of the eyes later.)

Cut the pineapple into quarters lengthwise. Cut out the core from each piece. Cut the pineapple into chunks or strips and place in a bowl. Toss fruit with 1 or 2 tablespoons clear or green crème de menthe. Cover and chill several hours, stirring occasionally to bring up juice from bottom of bowl. (If you prefer a sweeter dessert, sprinkle a little powdered sugar over the pineapple before adding the crème de menthe.)

Carry to picnic in chilled wide-mouth vacuum bottle or packed with cold foods.

Makes 6 servings

CHAMPAGNE BRUNCH

Citrus-Berry Bowl
Herbed Sausage Loaf
Hard-cooked Eggs
Croissants   Miniature Sweet Rolls
Apricot Preserves   Butter
Cheese Tray   Spiced Nuts
Champagne
Coffee

The idea of brunching outdoors while sipping the bubbly has great appeal but raises the question of how to serve eggs and sausage without a fire. The answer: with style!

Hard cook the eggs, of course, and slice them next to an elegant Herbed Sausage Loaf. This particular loaf combines good flavor and the ease of slicing of a terrine without the usual layers of fat. Like the rest of the menu, the loaf is prepared the day before so that making the big jug of coffee and packing up are the only tasks left for the morning of the brunch.

Citrus-Berry Bowl

2 large grapefruit
2 large navel oranges
1 tablespoon boiling water
2 tablespoons sugar
2 tablespoons fresh lime juice
1 kiwi fruit
Fresh mint leaves (optional)
1 quart fresh strawberries

Peel grapefruit and oranges and cut away all white membrane. Section fruit over a bowl to catch the juice. Set aside.

Stir boiling water into sugar. Continue to stir until sugar dissolves. Add lime juice and pour over grapefruit and orange sections. Peel and slice kiwi into fruit mixture. Cover and chill. Carry to picnic in insulated cooler.

Wash mint leaves and pat dry. Carry to picnic in plastic bag tucked in with the cold foods.

Wash and hull berries. Spread on paper toweling to dry. Cover lightly and store in refrigerator. Carry to picnic with cold foods. At serving time, slice strawberries into fruit mixture. Toss lightly to distribute berry slices and to coat fruit with syrup from bottom of bowl. Garnish with fresh mint.
Makes 8 servings

Herbed Sausage Loaf

1 10-ounce package frozen
    chopped spinach, thawed
2 pounds mildly seasoned fresh
    pork sausage meat
½ pound ground veal
½ cup finely chopped onion
1 slightly beaten egg
2 tablespoons white wine
½ teaspoon dried thyme,
    crushed
½ teaspoon dried basil, crushed

Drain spinach and squeeze out as much liquid as possible. Combine spinach with sausage, veal, and onion. Work with mixture until all ingredients are well distributed.

Combine egg, wine, thyme, and basil. Add to sausage mixture and blend until well distributed. Fry about 1 tablespoon of mixture in a small skillet until thoroughly cooked. Taste to check seasoning level. (Never taste raw sausage mixture.) Add salt or pepper as needed.

Pack mixture into a 9-by-5-by-3-inch loaf pan. Bake 60 to 70 minutes at 350°F. Near the end of the baking time, check the internal temperature of the loaf with a roast-meat thermometer. When the loaf is done, the thermometer will register 170°F.

Using a turkey (bulb) baster, remove accumulated fat from around the loaf. Leaving the loaf in the pan and while it is still hot, weight down loaf by placing another loaf pan on top and filling it with canned goods. Cool 1 hour.

Remove loaf from pan. Wrap in heavy-duty foil. Store in refrigerator overnight. Carry to picnic in an insulated cooler. Slice when ready to serve.

Makes 8 servings

Spiced Nuts

¼ cup water
¼ cup packed brown sugar
¼ cup granulated sugar
½ teaspoon ground cinnamon
¼ teaspoon ground nutmeg
2 cups walnut or pecan halves

Bring water, sugars, and spices to a full rolling boil. Boil 2 minutes; time closely. Remove from heat. Stir in nuts.

Immediately pour nuts onto a lightly buttered baking sheet. Working quickly with two forks, pull nuts apart.

When cool, store in tightly covered container.

Makes 2 cups

BEACH BASKET SPECIAL

Chutney-Cheese Spread
Apple Wedges   Celery Chunks
Curried Drumsticks
Hard Rolls   Butter
Banana-Nut Drops
Beer   Soft Drinks

The perfect scenario for a day at the beach would include a swim, a little sunbathing, and perhaps some volleyball, followed by a cool, crisp lunch. Unfortunately, the same sun that makes the first activities so pleasant can wilt the lunch at an alarming rate.

A smarter sequence is to feast first, then sunbathe and swim later. And, to be sure the food stays thoroughly chilled until the moment it is served, write into the script an ample cooler, well packed with ice.

Chutney-Cheese Spread

1 8-ounce package cream
    cheese, cubed and softened
½ teaspoon dry mustard
¼ cup Major Grey's chutney
Milk
Apples
Celery chunks

Beat cream cheese and mustard on medium speed of electric mixer. With kitchen scissors cut up large pieces of fruit in the chutney. Blend chutney into cream cheese.

Add milk, 1 tablespoon at a time, to make a spreading consistency. Transfer spread to small container with tight-fitting lid. Chill. Carry to picnic with cold foods.

Carry whole apples to picnic and cut into wedges when time to eat. Wash and cut up celery in advance and pack with cold foods.
Makes about ⅔ cup

Curried Drumsticks

1 cup finely crushed rich
   crackers
1 teaspoon curry powder
½ teaspoon salt
Dash cayenne
8 chicken drumsticks
¼ cup milk

Combine cracker crumbs, curry powder, salt, and cayenne. Dip drumsticks in milk and roll in crumb mixture. Arrange chicken in greased shallow pan. Bake, uncovered, in 375°F. oven about 1 hour. Chill. Carry to picnic in insulated cooler.
Makes 4 servings

Banana-Nut Drops

½ cup butter or margarine
1 cup packed brown sugar
1 egg
½ teaspoon vanilla
1 cup mashed very ripe banana
2¼ cups all-purpose flour
1 teaspoon baking powder
½ teaspoon baking soda
½ teaspoon ground cinnamon
¼ teaspoon salt
¼ cup sour cream
½ cup cashews or walnuts
Browned Butter Frosting (See
   recipe below)

Cream butter and brown sugar until light and fluffy. Add egg and beat well. Add vanilla and mashed banana.

Stir together flour, baking powder, soda, cinnamon, and salt. Stir into banana mixture alternately with sour cream. Stir in chopped nuts.

Drop by teaspoonfuls about 2 inches apart on ungreased baking sheet. Bake in 400°F. oven 8 to 10 minutes. *Note:* cookies will be only lightly browned. Remove from pan at once and cool on rack. Frost with Browned Butter Frosting. Store in tightly covered container.

Makes 4 dozen cookies

Browned Butter Frosting

3 tablespoons butter
2 cups sifted powdered sugar
2 tablespoons milk
1 teaspoon vanilla

Melt butter in a small heavy saucepan. Stir constantly over low heat until butter begins to brown. Remove from heat. Stir in powdered sugar, milk, and vanilla. Beat until smooth. Spread on cookies.

PARADE-WATCHER'S BOX LUNCH

Pita Bread
Swiss Cheese　Avocado
Alfalfa Sprouts
Nectarines　Green Grapes
Alice's Ginger Cookies
Homemade Lemonade
Red Wine

Come early and bring your lunch when staking out those curb-side seats for the big parade. Equip each member of your party with a share of the food and a folding chair. You can talk and eat comfortably while waiting for the blare of trumpets that signals the start of the parade.

Don't skimp on the niceties. A wine glass wrapped in a large cloth napkin doesn't weigh much in the lunch box and lets the rest of the crowd know you know how things should be done.

Pita Bread *(Bread with a Pocket)*

1 package active dry yeast
1 tablespoon sugar
1 teaspoon salt
3¼ to 3½ cups all-purpose flour
    (or substitute 1 cup whole
    wheat flour, if desired)
1¼ cups water
2 tablespoons cooking oil

In large mixer bowl combine yeast, sugar, salt, and 1½ cups of the flour. Heat water and oil until just warm (120°F.). Add to flour mixture. Blend ½ minute at low speed of electric mixer, scraping bowl constantly. Beat 3 minutes at high speed, scraping the bowl as necessary.

By hand add enough of remaining flour to make a firm dough. Knead 10 minutes on a floured surface until dough is smooth and elastic. Place in a greased bowl and turn dough greased side up. Cover and let rise in a warm place until double in bulk, about 1 hour.

Punch down dough. Turn onto lightly floured surface. Divide dough into 8 equal balls. Cover and let rise 30 minutes.

Place oven rack at next-to-lowest position. Depending on size of oven, lay one or more cake-cooling racks crosswise on the oven rack. (Pitas will be baked directly on these racks instead of on a pan.) Preheat oven to 500°F.

Roll each ball into a circle ¼-inch thick. Place 3 or 4 pitas on rack. Bake 5 to 7 minutes until puffed and golden brown. Remove from oven with a large pancake turner or tongs. Repeat with remaining balls.

Cool pitas on a rack. As soon as they are cool enough to handle, slit one end with a sharp knife. Store in plastic bags.
Makes 8 servings

Pita Sandwiches

Pita bread
Softened butter
Alfalfa sprouts
Swiss cheese
Avocado

Spread insides of pita bread with softened butter.

Wash alfalfa sprouts and drain on paper towels. Pack sprouts in a plastic bag with a crumpled paper towel in the bottom.

Take Swiss cheese to picnic in one chunk and slice it at lunchtime. Carry avocado whole; peel and cut up just in time to slip into the sandwiches.

Picnic Pointers: This lunch, beverages excepted, could indeed be packed in lunch boxes. However, if the day promises to be hot, the quality of the food will suffer. The sprouts may go limp and the cheese can become oily.

A better plan is to use one of the small insulated carriers and keep things cold with ice cubes sealed in a milk carton or plastic bowl with cover. This has the advantage of providing extra ice for the lemonade or water for finger washing.

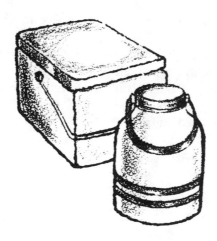

Alice's Ginger Cookies

½ cup butter or margarine
6 tablespoons sugar
¼ cup molasses
1 egg
2 cups all-purpose flour
½ teaspoon baking soda
½ teaspoon ground ginger
½ teaspoon ground cinnamon
Colored or coarse granulated
    sugar

Cream butter and sugar. Add molasses and egg and beat mixture well.

Stir together flour, baking soda, ginger, and cinnamon. Add to creamed mixture and beat well. Chill dough.

Roll chilled dough ⅛-inch thick on a lightly floured surface. Cut with cookie cutters. Place cookies on ungreased baking sheet. Sprinkle with colored sugar.

Bake in 375°F. oven 8 to 10 minutes, depending on the size of the cookie cutter used.

Makes 3½ to 4 dozen cookies

Homemade Lemonade

Skip the frozen concentrate and enjoy the flavor of fresh lemons and oranges. This version is slightly tart—a real thirst quencher.

FOR EACH QUART:
1 cup water
¾ cup sugar
½ cup freshly squeezed lemon
    juice
½ cup freshly squeezed orange
    juice
6 ice cubes
Ice-cold water

Heat 1 cup of water and sugar, stirring until sugar dissolves. Remove from heat. Cool. Add lemon and orange juices and chill.

Place 6 ice cubes in chilled vacuum bottle. Pour fruit syrup over ice and fill container with ice-cold water.

Makes 4 servings

CHICHI COMBINATION

Bloody Marys
Celery Stirrers
Spinach Quiche
Pickled Beet Slices
Cantaloupe or Honeydew Melon
Sparkling Water
Coffee

Repeated visits to a nearby picnic site require vigilance in planning to keep the menu from becoming repetitious, too. If standard picnic fare has been the pattern, switch to something chic and take advantage of being close to home by baking and taking a creamy Spinach Quiche. Pack tall glasses and longer celery stalks for the Bloody Marys. Choose solid colors of a fashionable hue for tablecloth and napkins.

Spinach Quiche

1 unbaked 9-inch pastry shell
   (See recipe below)
1 10-ounce package frozen
   spinach, thawed and well
   drained
1 tablespoon grated onion
4 eggs
2 cups light cream or half and
   half
1 teaspoon salt
⅛ teaspoon pepper
1½ cups shredded natural
   Swiss cheese
Nutmeg

Prepare pie shell according to recipe which follows. (If you prefer to use a pie crust mix, pick up instructions at the point of using foil and dried beans.)

Squeeze as much liquid as possible from spinach. Beat eggs slightly. Stir in spinach, cream, onion, salt, and pepper. Set aside.

Meanwhile, preheat over to 450°F. Bake pastry only 5 minutes. Remove from oven and turn oven temperature down to 325°F. Do not allow pastry to cool. Carefully remove foil and beans and save for another use.

Sprinkle cheese over bottom of hot pie shell. Pour custard mixture over cheese and sprinkle lightly with nutmeg. Protect edges of crust with 2-inch-wide strips of foil.

Return to oven. Bake 35 to 40 minutes until a knife inserted 1 inch from edge comes out clean. The center may still be soft, but it will set up after the quiche is out of the oven.

To serve hot: Set quiche as soon as it comes from the oven on a double thickness of heavy-duty foil. Close foil lightly around pie and transfer to insulated carrier. Serve within 2 hours.

To serve cold: Let quiche stand on rack 30 minutes. Cover lightly with foil and chill in refrigerator. Carry to picnic in an insulated cooler.

Makes 6 servings

Pastry for 9-inch Pie Shell

1 cup all-purpose flour
½ teaspoon salt
⅓ cup shortening
Cold milk

Stir together flour and salt. Cut shortening into flour with a pastry blender or two knives. Mixture should contain pieces the size of small peas.

Sprinkle milk, 1 tablespoon at a time, over flour. Toss flour mixture with a fork after each tablespoon of milk. After 2 tablespoons of milk have been used, try to gather dough together. If it doesn't hold a ball, sprinkle another tablespoon of milk over crumbly mixture and try again. Repeat if necessary. When dough can be compressed into a ball, let it rest 10 minutes.

Roll dough out on a lightly floured surface or pastry cloth. Make a circle 1½ inches larger than the rim of a 9-inch pie pan.

Fold circle into quarters and transfer to pie plate. Pat but do not stretch dough to fit pan. Trim overhanging edge of pastry 1 inch from rim of pan. Fold edge under and flute.

Do not prick crust. Instead, line the pie shell with a large piece of heavy-duty foil and fill with dried beans. Set aside while preparing filling ingredients for Spinach Quiche. Bake and fill as directed.

Makes 1 9-inch pie shell

Pickled Beet Slices

1 16-ounce can sliced beets
⅓ cup vinegar
1 tablespoon sugar
½ teaspoon ground cinnamon
¼ teaspoon ground allspice

Drain beets, reserving liquid. Add enough water to liquid to make 1 cup. Combine beet liquid, vinegar, sugar, cinnamon, and allspice. Bring to a boil. Stir in beets; bring to a boil again. Remove from heat. Chill beets in liquid; drain before serving. Carry to picnic in cooler with chilled sparking water.

Makes 6 servings

DINNER ON DECK

Gouda Cheese
Apple Wedges   Crackers
Corned Beef
Mustard Slaw
Dill Pickles   Rye Rolls
Rum-Raisin Bars
Beer   Coffee

Whether your craft is a yacht or a dinghy, the crew expects to dine from the captain's stores. Plan a pirate party around the refreshments that come aboard in insulated treasure chests. Have plenty of bandanas to use as place mats and neckerchiefs. After the meal, distribute gold foil-wrapped chocolate doubloons as part of the booty.

Corned Beef

Several types of corned beef are available to the picnicker. You may buy this flavorful meat precooked and sliced at a delicatessen. Pack your purchase with the other perishables in an insulated cooler.

Corned beef from the meat case is very easy to cook. A 2- to 3-pound piece would be ample for this picnic. If you have difficulty finding a piece this size, cook a larger piece and count on sandwiches another day. Remember, however, to carry only what you'll eat at the picnic and leave the rest at home in the refrigerator.

Most ready-to-cook corned beef comes already spiced. The seasonings may be loose in the package or in a separate packet. It is a matter of personal preference whether you decide to use them.

Cooking Directions: Remove meat from its vacuum package and place in a small kettle. Cover with water and bring liquid to a boil. Cover kettle and reduce heat. Simmer gently until the meat is fork tender. An hour per pound is a good rule of thumb unless the piece weighs more than 5 pounds, in which case the time may be slightly shorter. Test for doneness with a long-tined meat fork.

Let corned beef stand in cooking liquid 1 hour. Chill in refrigerator in liquid several hours or overnight. Before leaving for picnic, drain meat and wrap in heavy-duty foil. Carry to picnic in insulated cooler. Slice just before serving. If you plan to serve corned beef hot, wrap immediately after cooking in heavy-duty foil and pack in an insulated carrier.

Note: Corned beef labeled "for oven roasting" goes into a 350°F. oven on a rack in an open pan for the required cooking time. Specific directions will be packaged with the meat.

Mustard Slaw

4 cups chopped or finely
    shredded cabbage
¼ cup chopped green pepper
½ cup mayonnaise or salad
    dressing
¼ cup sour cream
2 teaspoons Dijon mustard
2 teaspoons cider vinegar
½ teaspoon salt

Toss cabbage and green pepper. Chill in a covered container.

Blend together mayonnaise, sour cream, mustard, vinegar, and salt. Chill in covered container.

Carry vegetables and dressing to picnic with cold foods. Toss just before serving.

Makes 6 servings

Rum-Raisin Bars

½ cup dark or light rum
2 tablespoons butter or
    margarine
¾ cup raisins
1¼ cups all-purpose flour
2 tablespoons packed brown
    sugar
½ cup butter or margarine
2 eggs
¾ cup packed brown sugar
½ cup chopped walnuts

Heat rum and butter until butter melts. Pour mixture over raisins. Set aside.

Mix flour and the 2 tablespoons brown sugar. Cut in butter and press into a 9-inch-square pan. Bake in 350°F. oven for 15 minutes.

Beat eggs slightly. Stir in remaining brown sugar, nuts, and rum-raisin mixture. Pour over baked layer.

Bake at 350°F. for 20 to 25 minutes. Cut into bars while still warm.

Makes 24 bars

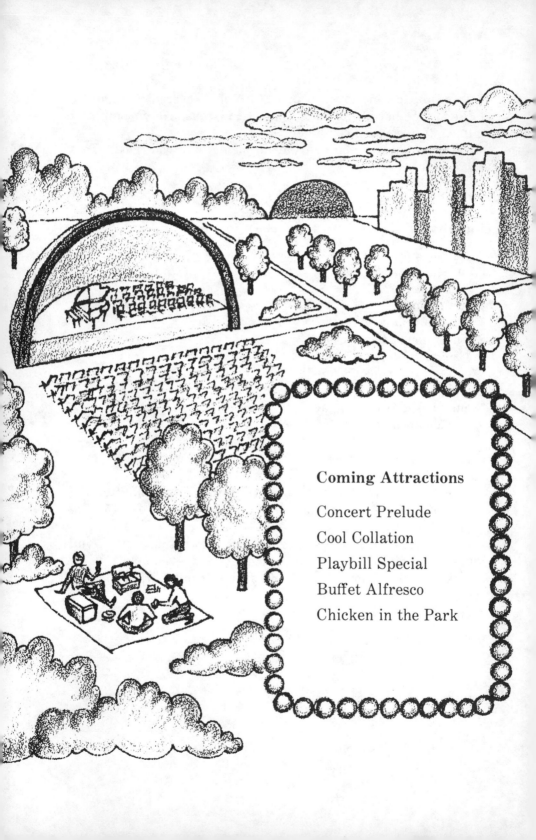

Coming Attractions

Concert Prelude
Cool Collation
Playbill Special
Buffet Alfresco
Chicken in the Park

2

Posh Little Suppers

Come summer, every conceivable type of cultural event moves outdoors. Opera companies, symphony orchestras, theater casts, groups, and soloists book themselves into tents, pavilions, and open-air stages across the country. The talent may be local or big name in quality, but along with entertainment, each performance presents a picnic possibility.

Not only does this offer a pleasant, unhurried way to dine before the show, but it also provides infinitely better food than is usually available either close at hand or on the premises. And since in many communities these entertainments are accessible by public transportation or chartered bus, a picnic supper is made to order for this convenient option.

People who consider fine food a cultural event in its own right don't wait for a visiting road show before staging a picnic on a long, day-lit evening or under the stars. They know that simple foods, elegantly presented, win applause from their own devoted following.

CONCERT PRELUDE

Ratatouille   Crackers
Pâté Loaf
Brioches   Butter
Fresh Strawberries
Sour Cream   Brown Sugar
Red Wine
Coffee

Ratatouille

2 cups coarsely chopped onion
2 small cloves garlic, minced
2 tablespoons olive oil or
    cooking oil
4 medium tomatoes, coarsely
    chopped
2 zucchini, halved lengthwise
    and cut into ½-inch slices
    (about 8 ounces)
1 small unpeeled eggplant,
    diced
1 green pepper, cut into
    julienne strips
1 teaspoon salt
⅛ teaspoon freshly ground
    pepper
2 or 3 fresh basil leaves,
    snipped, or 1 teaspoon
    dried basil leaves, crushed
2 sprigs fresh thyme, snipped,
    or ½ teaspoon dried thyme
    leaves, crushed

In a large skillet cook onion and garlic in oil until tender but not brown. Add remaining ingredients and toss gently to distribute the onions.

Bring mixture to a boil. Cover pan and reduce heat. Simmer gently 35 minutes. Stir occasionally, taking care not to break up vegetable pieces any more than necessary. Taste mixture. Add salt or pepper as needed.

Simmer, uncovered, for 5 to 10 minutes to reduce the amount of liquid. Remove from heat and let stand at room temperature about 20 minutes. Transfer to covered container and chill thoroughly. Carry to picnic in insulated cooler.

Makes 6 servings

Pâté Loaf

2 slightly beaten eggs
2 tablespoons brandy
1 teaspoon dried marjoram,
    crushed
½ teaspoon salt
⅛ teaspoon pepper
1 cup fine soft bread crumbs
1 pound ground beef round
    steak
8 ounces braunschweiger,
    softened

In a mixing bowl combine eggs, brandy, marjoram, salt, and pepper. Stir in bread crumbs.

Combine ground round steak and softened braunschweiger until the latter is well distributed.

Add meat to egg mixture. Mix thoroughly. Pack meat loaf into an 8½-by-4½-by-2½-inch loaf pan. Bake at 350°F. for 50 to 60 minutes. Let stand 1 hour. Carefully remove loaf from pan. Wrap in foil and refrigerate several hours or overnight. Carry to picnic in insulated cooler. Slice at serving time.

Makes 6 servings

Brioches

1 package active dry yeast
¾ cup warm water
    (105–115°F.)
½ cup sugar
½ teaspoon salt
3 eggs
1 egg yolk (reserve white)
½ cup butter or margarine,
    softened
3½ cups all-purpose flour

In a large mixer bowl dissolve yeast in warm water. Add sugar, salt, eggs, egg yolk, butter, and 2 cups of the flour. Beat ½ minute at low speed of electric mixer, scraping the bowl constantly. Beat 10 minutes at medium speed, scraping the bowl as necessary.

Stir in remaining flour by hand. Beat until smooth. Scrape batter from sides of bowl. Cover and let rise in a warm place until double in bulk, about 1 hour.

Stir down batter by beating 25 strokes. Cover the bowl lightly and refrigerate at least 8 hours.

Stir down batter. Divide in half. Place one half on lightly floured surface. Return other half to the refrigerator. Roll dough into a roll about 8 inches long. Cut into 16 slices with a thread. (Lay a piece of white thread under roll at place where dough is to be sliced. Cross ends of thread and slowly pull ends as though tieing a knot. Thread will cut dough.)

With well-floured hands shape 12 slices into balls and place each in a greased muffin cup. Dough is soft and sticky. Flatten tops and made a deep indentation in the center of each ball.

Cut each of remaining 4 slices into 3 equal parts. Shape each into a small ball, roll lightly in flour and place atop indentation. Repeat with remaining dough. Let rise until double, about 40 minutes.

Beat reserved egg white slightly. Brush over rolls. Bake in 375°F. oven 15 to 20 minutes.
Makes 24 rolls

Fresh Strawberries with Sour Cream and Brown Sugar

1 quart fresh strawberries
1 cup sour cream
1 cup brown sugar

Select the most beautiful berries you can find. Leaving the hulls on, wash fruit carefully and spread on paper toweling to dry. Cover lightly and store in the refrigerator. Carry to picnic with cold foods.

Pack sour cream with cold foods. Spoon into a small bowl before serving.

Carry brown sugar to picnic in a tightly covered container. Transfer to a small bowl at serving time.

Invite guests to dip tip of a strawberry into sour cream and then into brown sugar before eating.

Makes 6 servings

COOL COLLATION

Kir
Smoked Almonds
Poached Red Snapper
Carrots and Pea Fods
Buttered Parker House Rolls
Orange-Chocolate Cookies
White Wine
Coffee

Kir

Novels with a continental setting sometimes depict one or more of the main characters sipping a Kir while engaging in smart conversation. You are on your own for the witty words, but the combination of black currant liqueur and white wine makes a delightful predinner drink.

FOR EACH DRINK:
1 tablespoon crème de cassis
6 ounces dry white wine,
    chilled
Ice cubes (optional)

Premix appropriate multiples of the ingredients (except ice) and carry to picnic in prechilled vacuum jug. Or, carry crème de cassis and wine separately in an ice chest and mix drinks to order at the picnic.

Picnic pointer: Pack a container of ice cubes in the cooler with the chilled wine for the meal. They not only assist with the cooling, but also will be available for those who want the Kir on the rocks.

Poached Red Snapper

1 carrot, finely chopped
1 stalk celery, finely chopped
1 small onion, sliced
6 whole peppercorns
½ teaspoon salt
4 serving-sized red snapper
    fillets
¼ cup dry white wine
Water
Snipped parsley
Lemon wedges

Spread carrots, celery, and onions in 12-inch skillet. Add peppercorns and sprinkle with salt.

Lay red snapper fillets skin side down on top of the vegetables. Pour wine over fish and add enough water so that liquid just covers fish.

Bring liquid to a boil and immediately turn heat down so that liquid barely simmers. Cover skillet and cook until flesh becomes translucent and fish flakes easily when tested with a fork. This will take 5 to 8 minutes. Watch time carefully so that fish is not overcooked.

Lift fish out of cooking liquid with slotted spatula. Place each portion on a piece of heavy-duty foil. Sprinkle with parsley. Let cool 30 minutes. Close foil packets and chill thoroughly. Take to picnic in insulated cooler. Serve with lemon wedges.
Makes 4 servings

Picnic pointer: Before leaving home tie each lemon wedge in a small square of cheesecloth. This will strain the juice as wedge is being squeezed over fish at serving time. Pack in a plastic bag or sealed container and place with cold foods.

Carrots and Pea Pods

4 medium carrots
1 6-ounce package frozen pea
    pods, thawed
French dressing

Bias slice carrots about ½ inch thick. Simmer in a covered saucepan in ½ inch boiling salted water for 6 to 8 minutes. Pieces should be crisp-tender, not soft. Drain well.

Rinse pea pods in boiling water. Drain well. Toss with cooked carrots. Toss vegetables with enough French dressing to coat lightly. Refrigerate in covered container. Carry to picnic with cold foods. Toss again just before serving.

Makes 4 servings

Orange-Chocolate Cookies

1 cup sugar
⅓ cup cooking oil
2 1-ounce squares unsweetened
    chocolate, melted and
    cooled
2 tablespoons frozen orange
    juice concentrate,
    undiluted
1 tablespoon orange-flavored
    liqueur
3 eggs
1½ cups all-purpose flour
1½ teaspoons baking powder
Chocolate shot

Combine sugar, oil, and melted chocolate. Stir in orange juice concentrate and liqueur. Add eggs one at a time, beating well after each addition.

Stir together flour and baking powder. Blend into chocolate mixture. Beat well. Chill dough.

Shape dough into 1-inch balls. Dip tops in chocolate shot. Place on ungreased baking sheet. Bake at 375°F. 10 to 12 minutes. Remove from baking sheet at once. Cool on a rack. Store in tightly covered container.

Makes 3 dozen cookies

PLAYBILL SPECIAL

Mushroom Consommé
Peppered Sirloin Steak
Romaine   Blue Cheese Dressing
Sliced Tomatoes
Lemon-Berry Meringues
White Wine
Coffee

Mushroom Consommé

2 10½-ounce cans condensed
    beef consommé
2 cups water
½ pound fresh mushrooms,
    thinly sliced
¼ cup dry sherry or white wine

Place consommé, water, and mushrooms in heavy saucepan. Simmer, covered, for 1 hour. Remove mushrooms with a slotted spoon and discard.

Add wine to consommé. Bring mixture to a boil and transfer to heated 1-quart vacuum bottle.
Makes 4 servings

Peppered Sirloin Steak

1¾ pounds sirloin steak, cut at
    least 1-inch thick
Salt
Coarsely ground black pepper

Place meat on a rack in a broiler pan. Slash fat around the edge at several points, taking care not to cut into the meat. Do not season.

Preheat broiler and place broiler pan so that the surface of the meat is 2 to 3 inches from the heat.

Broil until top of the meat is browned, about 10 minutes. Season top lightly with salt and generously with pepper. Turn meat with tongs. Broil 8 minutes. Season second side with salt and pepper.

Let meat stand 20 minutes. Transfer to a large piece of heavy-duty foil. Wrap steak and carry to picnic in an insulated cooler. *Note:* if not leaving for picnic immediately, store foil-wrapped steak in refrigerator until ready to pack food. Cut steak into thin strips across the grain at serving time.
Makes 4 servings

Lemon-Berry Meringues

1 egg
1 egg yolk (reserve white)
¼ cup sugar
¼ cup lemon juice
1 tablespoon butter
¼ teaspoon grated lemon peel
¼ teaspoon cream of tartar
¼ teaspoon vanilla
Dash salt
⅓ cup sugar (for meringue)
Strawberries for garnish

To make filling: In small saucepan beat egg and egg yolk well. Blend in sugar, lemon juice, and butter. Cook over low heat, stirring constantly, until thickened and bubbly, about 10 minutes. Remove from heat. Stir in lemon peel. Chill in covered container. Carry to picnic with cold foods.

To make meringues: Have reserved egg white at room temperature in a small mixing bowl. Add cream of tartar, vanilla, and salt. Beat until soft peaks form.

Add sugar gradually until very stiff peaks form and sugar is dissolved. Do not underbeat.

Draw four circles, 3 inches in diameter, on a piece of foil or brown paper. Lay foil on ungreased baking sheet. Shape one-fourth of mixture into a shell on each circle. (For an extra-fancy look, pipe mixture through pastry tube using a star tip.) Build up edges so center has indentation.

Bake in 300°F. oven for 40 minutes. Turn off heat and let meringues dry in oven another 40 minutes without opening door. Cool on a rack. Take to picnic in ventilated carrier.

To assemble desserts: Spoon one-fourth of lemon filling into each meringue shell. Garnish with sliced strawberries.

Makes 4 servings

BUFFET ALFRESCO

Cheeses   Cracker Basket
Ham Loaf en Croûte
Stuffed Tomatoes
Fresh Fruit   Chinese Chews
Rosé Wine
Coffee

Ham Loaf en Croûte

3 slightly beaten eggs
½ cup sour cream
¼ cup finely chopped onion
1 tablespoon prepared
    horseradish
3 cups fine soft bread crumbs
1½ pounds ground fully cooked
    ham
½ pound ground veal
1 package frozen patty shells
1 well beaten egg

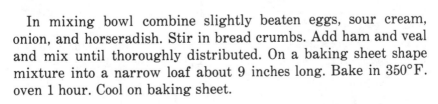

In mixing bowl combine slightly beaten eggs, sour cream, onion, and horseradish. Stir in bread crumbs. Add ham and veal and mix until thoroughly distributed. On a baking sheet shape mixture into a narrow loaf about 9 inches long. Bake in 350°F. oven 1 hour. Cool on baking sheet.

Thaw dough for frozen patty shells. Roll dough on a lightly floured surface into a rectangle large enough to enclose the meat loaf.

Place loaf top side down on dough and wrap around loaf. Edges should overlap enough to seal, but excess should be trimmed away. Save trimmings to decorate top of loaf. Seal edges of pastry with beaten egg. Turn loaf right side up on baking sheet.

Roll trimmings into two long strips to crisscross over top of loaf or make other small decorations as desired. Place decorations on loaf and brush with beaten egg.

Preheat oven to 400°F. Bake about 35 minutes or until golden brown.

To serve hot: As soon as loaf comes from the oven, transfer it to a large sheet of heavy-duty foil and wrap loosely. Carry to picnic in an insulated carrier. Slice at serving time.

To serve cold: Remove loaf to rack. Let stand 20 minutes. Wrap in foil and store in refrigerator until chilled thoroughly. Carry to picnic in insulated cooler. Slice at serving time.

Makes 8 servings

Stuffed Tomatoes

8 medium tomatoes
1 small cucumber
2 tablespoons thinly sliced
    green onion with tops
Salt
Dill weed

Plunge tomatoes, one at a time, into boiling water for about 20 seconds to loosen skin. Beginning at stem end, peel tomatoes. Cut out center core, being careful not to cut all the way through the bottom of the tomato.

Turn tomatoes upside down in a colander or on a rack to drain. Place drained tomatoes in a covered container and chill.

Peel, seed, and finely chop cucumber to make about ¾ cup. Toss with green onion, salt, and dill weed to taste. Store in covered container in the refrigerator. Carry to picnic with cold foods.

When ready to serve tomatoes, spoon some of the cucumber mixture into the cavity of each tomato. Tomatoes may be cut partway through in sixths to open wider for a flower effect, if desired.

Makes 8 servings

Chinese Chews

¾ cup all-purpose flour
¾ cup sugar
½ teaspoon baking powder
1 cup chopped dates
1 cup finely chopped walnuts
2 well-beaten eggs
Granulated sugar

In mixing bowl stir together flour, sugar, and baking powder. Add dates, nuts, and eggs. Mix well to moisten dry ingredients.

Pat mixture into greased and floured 9-inch-square pan. Bake at 350°F. for 25 to 27 minutes. Cut into squares. While still warm, quickly roll each piece into a ball. Roll in granulated sugar. Store in tightly covered container.

Makes 3 dozen cookies

CHICKEN IN THE PARK

Prosciutto with Melon
Oven-Fried Sesame Chicken
Mixed Greens Salad
Ricotta Cheesecake
Sangria Blanca
Coffee

Prosciutto with Melon

Wrap thin slices of prosciutto around cantaloupe or honeydew melon cubes. Fasten with cocktail picks. Chill. Carry to picnic in ice chest.

Oven-Fried Sesame Chicken

½ cup butter
1 beaten egg
½ cup milk
1 cup all-purpose flour
¼ cup toasted sesame seeds
1½ teaspoons salt
1 teaspoon paprika
Chicken thighs, drumsticks,
    and split breasts to make 8
    servings

Melt butter in a shallow baking pan in 400°F. oven. When butter is melted but not browned, remove from oven.

Place egg and milk in pie plate or other flat dish.

Shake flour, sesame seeds, paprika, and pepper in plastic bag.

Dip chicken pieces into egg mixture and then into seasoned flour. Place chicken pieces in baking pan, turning to coat with butter, and arrange skin side down in the pan in a single layer.

Bake at 400°F. for 30 minutes. Turn and bake another 30 minutes.

To serve hot: If feasible, wrap pan with foil and then in several layers of newspaper. Cover outside with a heavy towel or carry to picnic in insulated carrier.

To serve cold: Let chicken cool in pan 30 minutes. Transfer pieces to covered container and chill in refrigerator. Carry to picnic in insulated cooler.

Makes 8 servings

Ricotta Cheesecake

Less rich and less sweet, but oh so good

1 tablespoon sugar
¾ cup crushed graham cracker
    crumbs
1 tablespoon butter or
    margarine, melted
3 tablespoons dried currants
2 egg whites
2 tablespoons sugar
8 ounces ricotta cheese
2 egg yolks
½ teaspoon grated lemon peel
1 tablespoon lemon juice
1 teaspoon vanilla
2 tablespoons sugar
½ teaspoon salt
½ cup all-purpose flour
½ cup light cream

Stir sugar and crumbs into melted butter. Pat crumb mixture into bottom and up sides of an 8-inch pie pan. Sprinkle currants over crumbs.

Beat egg whites to soft peaks. Gradually add 2 tablespoons of sugar and beat to stiff peaks. Set meringue aside.

In mixing bowl cream ricotta, egg yolks, lemon peel, lemon juice, vanilla, sugar, and salt until smooth. Blend in flour. Add cream and mix until smooth. Fold in meringue.

Pour mixture into crumb crust. Bake in 325°F. oven about 45 minutes or until knife inserted off center comes out clean. (*Note*: Mixture will puff up slightly during baking but will settle back into crust after it is cooled.)

Chill cheesecake and carry to picnic in insulated cooler.
Makes 6 servings

Sangria Blanca

1 lime
2 lemons
2 oranges
½ cup sugar
¼ cup brandy
2 bottles dry white wine (750
　　ml. each)
1 32-ounce bottle sparkling
　　water
Ice cubes

Slice the lime and one of the lemons into thin cartwheel slices. With a sharp knife cut the outer peel of one of the oranges into a long spiral strip without any white membrane. Place sliced fruit and peel in a 1-quart jar with a screw-top lid.

Extract juice from remaining lemon and both oranges. Pour over fruit. Add sugar and brandy and stir until sugar dissolves. Cover and chill thoroughly. Carry to picnic in ice chest.

Chill wine and sparkling water in refrigerator. Carry to picnic in ice chest with container of ice cubes.

To serve: Transfer half of the fruit and fruit juices to a pitcher, preferably glass. Add 1 bottle of wine; stir to combine. Add half of sparkling water. Place 1 or 2 ice cubes in each glass. Pour Sangria over ice. Repeat with remaining ingredients.
Makes 8 servings

Dining Itinerary

Le Bon Pique-nique
Viking Table
Italian Merenda
Greek Taverna Supper
Sultan's Tray
Oriental Medley
Mexican Fiesta
Canadian Fling

PASSPORT

3

International Accents

You don't have to be fluent in French, Italian, Greek, or any other foreign language in order to translate the joys of international cookery into unique picnic fare. Enthusiastic enjoyment of every last morsel speaks for itself.

The eight-menu package tour in this chapter includes six culinary stopovers in Europe, the Middle East, and the Orient, plus two in North America. For all the territory covered there's no jet lag to worry about in packing these delicacies off to a favorite park or nearby lake. Nor is matched luggage required. Insulated coolers and vacuum jugs do the job nicely.

Some of the foods are picnic standbys in their homelands while others have been borrowed or adapted especially for the outdoor scene. Each retains the character and flavor of its place of origin. Serving suggestions or interesting conversation tidbits accompany each menu.

LE BON PIQUE-NIQUE

Pâté Maison
Chicken Breasts Chaud-Froid
French Rolls   Butter
Spinach-Mushroom Salad
Camembert Cheese
Fresh Pears
Champagne   Coffee

The French not only gave us the word for picnic, but also many of the notions about what should be served. To be sure, people had carried lunches to work in the fields for as long as there had been lunches to carry and fields to farm. *Le pique-nique* turned the meal into an elegant country party.

Pâté Maison

1 8-ounce package cream
    cheese
½ cup chopped onion
¼ cup chopped celery
¼ cup water
2 teaspoons chicken bouillon
    granules
1 teaspoon salt
⅛ teaspoon pepper
1 pound calves' or baby beef
    liver
1 tablespoon prepared
    horseradish
Snipped parsley
Melba toast

Cut cream cheese into cubes and set aside at room temperature to soften.

In saucepan cook onion and celery in water with bouillon granules, salt, and pepper until vegetables are tender. Pour mixture into blender container.

Broil liver on well-oiled broiler pan just until firm and all of the pink is gone. Watch carefully and do not overcook. Liver should be moist and tender. Cut up liver and add to vegetables in blender container.

Add softened cream cheese and horseradish to blender container. Cover and process mixture a few seconds. Stop blender and push contents away from sides with rubber spatula. Repeat several times until mixture is smooth. Watch texture carefully. Overblending will turn mixture to a liquid.

Transfer mixture to 4 oiled custard cups. Refrigerate 24 hours. Cover custard cups with foil and take 2 or 3 of the molds to picnic in insulated cooler. At serving time loosen pâté with spatula and unmold on serving plate. Sprinkle generously with parsley, patting gently to be sure parsley sticks to surface. Serve with melba toast.

Makes about 2⅔ cups

Chicken Breasts Chaud-Froid

A take-along version of the classic dish, whose name comes from a sauce that is first hot and then cold.

6 chicken breasts, skinned,
    boned, and split
2 to 3 cups boiling chicken
    broth (if starting with
    bouillon cubes, add 1
    chopped carrot and 1
    chopped celery stalk with
    leaves)
1 cup milk or light cream
¼ cup butter
3 tablespoons all-purpose flour
Salt
White pepper
2½ to 3½ envelopes unflavored
    gelatin
Canned whole pimiento
Ripe olives

Arrange chicken breasts in bottom of a large heavy skillet. Tuck thin ends of meat underneath so pieces are fairly uniform in shape. Pour enough of the boiling broth over chicken to cover. Watching closely, heat until broth comes to a boil again. Immediately reduce heat so liquid simmers gently. Cover pan and simmer over low heat 12 to 15 minutes or until chicken is done.

Let chicken cool in liquid 1 hour. Lift pieces out of pan with slotted spoon, reserving broth. Arrange chicken pieces on a serving platter and chill in the refrigerator.

Strain reserved broth through cheesecloth or a fine sieve. When chicken is thoroughly chilled, heat 1 cup of the reserved broth and the milk.

In a saucepan melt butter and stir in flour, but do not let it brown. Add hot broth and milk all at once. Cook, stirring constantly, until thickened and bubbly. Season to taste with salt and white pepper.

Soften 2½ envelopes of gelatin (use only 2 if not for a picnic) in another ¼ cup of reserved chicken broth. Blend into hot sauce. Cook, stirring constantly, until gelatin is melted. Remove from heat and cool sauce, stirring occasionally to prevent a skin from forming on the surface. Chill in refrigerator or set saucepan in a pan of ice water. When sauce will coat a spoon lightly, remove from refrigerator or ice water.

Spoon a layer of sauce over each piece of chicken. Return chicken to refrigerator. Return sauce to refrigerator. When first layer has set, repeat. Do this three or four times or until sauce is used up. *Note*: Add last layer and decorate one piece at a time. If sauce gets too thick, heat slightly until it is the right consistency again.

To decorate: Drain pimiento. Cut into 12 thin strips and pat as dry as possible with paper toweling. Cut ripe olives into small pieces that look like flower petals. While last coating of sauce is still soft, place a strip of pimiento lengthwise on the chicken in a graceful stem or swirl. Press into soft sauce to anchor. Arrange ripe olive pieces along the pimiento strip in a decorative fashion. Press into soft surface to anchor. Return to the refrigerator and chill.

To glaze: (Although few chefs would omit this step, you may choose to do so. If you have pressed the decorations well into the sauce before it set, they will stay in place.)

Examine the remaining strained chicken broth closely. It must be absolutely clear or it will look cloudy over the chicken. If there is any doubt about the clarity, save for another purpose and make some broth from a chicken bouillon cube in ¾ cup boiling water. Soften the remaining envelope of gelatin in ¼ cup of cold water. Blend into hot broth and stir until melted. Chill, stirring occasionally until the mixture is the consistency of egg white. Spoon glaze over chicken pieces. Chill. Carry to picnic in insulated cooler.

Makes 6 servings

Spinach-Mushroom Salad

1½ pounds fresh spinach
½ pound fresh mushrooms
2 green onions, thinly sliced
⅔ cup olive oil or salad oil
¼ cup wine vinegar
2 tablespoons sugar
2 tablespoons toasted sesame
    seed

Wash spinach and pat dry. Tear spinach into bite-sized pieces into a plastic bag with a crumpled paper towel in the bottom. Close bag and chill. Carry to picnic with cold foods.

Wash mushrooms and pat dry. Carry to picnic in plastic bag in cooler. Slice just before serving and toss with spinach in salad bowl.

Combine oil, vinegar, sugar and sesame seed in screw-top jar. Chill. Just before serving shake well and toss with salad ingredients.

Makes 6 servings

VIKING TABLE

Pickled Herring
Smoked Salmon
Cold Sliced Pork or Veal Roast
Sliced Salami or Potato Sausage
Norwegian Celery and Apple Salad
Cheese
Rye Bread   Butter
Fresh Plum Soup with Sour Cream
Almond Cookie Squares
White Wine   Coffee

What's best about a smorgasbord, that assortment of tasty foods all served at once, translates deliciously into picnic fare. At first glance the menu seems complicated. But look again. You prepare the cold roast, the salad, the fruit soup, and the cookies. Everything else comes from the deli counter or bake shop.

Pork or Veal Roast

The day before the picnic place a 3-pound boneless pork or veal roast on a rack in an open pan. If the veal roast is unusually lean, lay two or three slices of bacon lengthwise on top of the meat.

Insert a meat thermometer in the center of the meat. Be sure the tip of the thermometer is in the meat and not resting in a seam where muscles in the boneless roast come together.

Set the oven thermostat at 325°F. There is no need to preheat the oven. Roast the meat, uncovered, for 1¾ to 2 hours or until the meat thermometer registers 170°F.

Remove roast from the oven and let stand 1 hour. Wrap roast in foil and refrigerate. Carry to picnic in an insulated cooler. Slice just before serving.

Picnic pointer: A 3-pound boneless pork or veal roast will provide 8 to 10 generous servings. If your picnic group is smaller, leave 1 or 2 portions of meat at home. In effect you are removing the leftovers first instead of toting them to and from the picnic and perhaps wasting them.

Fresh Plum Soup

Is it an appetizer or a dessert? In the Scandinavian countries fruit soup is as apt to be one course as the other in the menu.

2 pounds dark red plums
1 quart water
½ cup sugar
1 tablespoon lemon juice
1 to 2 inches stick cinnamon
2 tablespoons cornstarch
¼ to ½ cup white wine
½ cup sour cream

Wash plums but do not remove skins. Cut into halves and take out stones. Cut fruit into quarters. In saucepan simmer plums, water, sugar, lemon juice, and cinnamon until fruit is very tender, about 10 minutes. Discard cinnamon stick.

Press fruit through food mill or coarse sieve. Mix cornstarch with cold water and stir into plum purée. Bring mixture to a boil and simmer, stirring constantly, about 5 minutes. Taste soup for sweetness and to be sure no uncooked cornstarch flavor remains.

Remove soup from heat. Stir in wine.

To serve hot: Pour soup into heated 1-quart vacuum bottle.

To serve cold: Chill soup and pour into chilled 1-quart vacuum bottle.

Serve in heatproof glass punch cups. Top each serving with a dollop of sour cream, which was packed with the cold foods.

Makes 8 servings

Norwegian Celery and Apple Salad

4 cups coarsely sliced celery
¼ cup water
2 hard-cooked eggs, halved
    lengthwise
2 tablespoons cooking oil
2 tablespoons milk
1 tablespoon cider vinegar
1 teaspoon sugar
¾ teaspoon salt
⅛ teaspoon white pepper
2 tart red apples
Lettuce leaves for salad bowl

Simmer celery and water in covered saucepan until celery is crisp-tender, about 5 minutes. Stir occasionally. Do not overcook. Drain celery and chill in covered container. Carry to picnic with cold foods.

In a small mixing bowl mash hard-cooked egg yolks with oil to make a smooth paste. Blend in milk. Stir in vinegar, sugar, salt, and pepper until smooth and thoroughly distributed. Refrigerate dressing in covered jar. Pack with cold foods.

Wash lettuce leaves in cold water. Shake off excess moisture. Carry to picnic in plastic bag with crumpled paper towel in the bottom. Pack in cooler with other salad ingredients.

Wash and dry apples. Wait to chop apples until you are ready to toss the salad. Peel apples or not as you prefer.

Just before serving toss celery and chopped apple with the dressing. Spoon mixture into lettuce-lined salad bowl. Garnish with chopped hard-cooked egg white.

Makes 8 to 10 servings

Picnic pointer: To save space, tuck cooked egg whites in with the celery. Chop them when needed to garnish the salad.

Pickled Herring and Smoked Salmon

Purchase these delicacies at the delicatessen or refrigerated food section of the market. This time choose the herring without cream. The reason—sour cream will be served with the plum soup.

Salami or Potato Sausage

Fortunate cooks will have access to a Swedish meat market, from which you can buy potato sausage or other traditional sausages that may or may not need to be simmered before serving. The butcher on duty can tell you which.

Just as practical for a picnic, however, are sliced hard salami, thuringer, or other dry sausage. Summer sausage is another possibility. Allow two slices per person in your party. Unless you buy vacuum-packaged meats, rewrap your purchase in foil when you get home. Store in the refrigerator and keep cold in transit to the picnic.

Cheese

Do limit yourself to only one or two kinds of cheese for this Scandinavian meal. Restraint is difficult when confronted with the tempting array at the cheese counter. However, more variety isn't necessary and only adds to the number of items carried to and from the picnic ground.

Which one or two? Since the herring and the salmon have concentrated flavors, you should look for a cheese with broad appeal. A mild Tilset would complement the other foods. So would a baby Gouda or Edam. The latter two have protective wax coverings and can hold up well when jostled. Make the second cheese either a traditional goat cheese or one of the caraway-seeded varieties.

Whatever your choice, cheese rides best in the insulated cooler or ice chest. Since most picnics are summer affairs, the cheese will reach room temperature, in this case outdoor temperature, very quickly at the site.

Almond Cookie Squares

1½ cups all-purpose flour
⅓ cup sugar
½ teaspoon baking powder
½ teaspoon salt
½ cup butter
Milk
1 teaspoon vanilla
¼ teaspoon almond extract
1 8-ounce can almond paste

Stir together flour, sugar, baking powder, and salt. Cut in butter until crumbled particles are fine.

Combine 2 tablespoons milk with vanilla and almond extract. Toss with crumb mixture. Remove ¾ cup of mixture and set it aside.

Stir another 1 or 2 tablespoons of milk into remaining crumb mixture to make a soft cookie dough. Press dough into bottom of ungreased 9-inch-square pan.

Divide almond paste into 4 sections. Roll, pat, or otherwise shape each quarter into a 3-inch square. Place each square in one corner of the pan. Squares should meet in the center. (Don't worry if the squares tear or are slightly uneven. This is just the easiest way to shape the almond paste into a layer.)

Sprinkle reserved crumbled mixture over the almond paste. Press lightly with fingers to be sure almond paste layer is covered.

Bake in 350°F. oven 25 to 30 minutes or until top crumbs are light golden brown. Cut into squares as soon as pan comes from the oven.

Makes 16 squares

ITALIAN MERENDA

Antipasto Plate
Vitello Tonnato
Italian Bread   Butter
Macaroon-Topped Peaches
White Wine
Coffee

Not all great Italian masters are painters or musicians. Many of them are inspired cooks whose creations evoke pleasure and acclaim the world over. Pizza is perhaps the most famous export, but dishes such as Vitella Tonnato have their own international reputations.

Antipasto Plate

Hard-cooked egg wedges
Sliced pepperoni
Marinated artichokes
Olives
Italian peppers
Cherry tomatoes
Gorgonzola or blue cheese
    wedges

Hard cook the eggs yourself and purchase the rest of the items far enough ahead of the picnic so that they can be chilled in the refrigerator before packing in the insulated cooler. Slice the eggs and open the packages at serving time and arrange the foods on a large wooden plate.

Vitello Tonnato

2 pounds boneless veal roast,
    rolled and tied
½ cup white wine
Water
1 tablespoon wine vinegar
1 teaspoon salt
½ teaspoon dried sage, crushed
¼ cup olive oil
¼ cup cooking oil
¼ cup lemon juice
¼ cup white wine
4 anchovy fillets
1 6½-ounce can tuna, drained
2 tablespoons capers, drained

Place meat in a deep saucepan just wide enough to accommodate the meat with no more than an inch at either end. Pour ½ cup wine over the roast and add enough water just to cover meat. Add wine vinegar, salt, and sage. Bring liquid to a boil and reduce heat to a gentle simmer. Cover pan and cook 1½ hours. Add more water to keep meat covered during cooking time, if necessary.

Remove meat from cooking liquid and let stand about 15 minutes. Carve into at least 12 thin slices. Arrange slices on serving platter.

In blender container place olive oil, cooking oil, lemon juice, and ¼ cup wine. Add anchovies and tuna. Blend until smooth.

Spoon sauce over meat, making sure all surfaces are covered. Sprinkle capers over top. Refrigerate, uncovered, for about 1 hour until sauce has set. Cover platter with foil and chill several hours or overnight. Carry to picnic in insulated cooler.

Makes 6 servings

Macaroon-Topped Peaches

A portable version of an Italian favorite.

2 tablespoons butter
¼ cup sugar
¼ teaspoon almond extract
1 well-beaten egg
1 cup crumbled macaroons
6 firm, ripe peaches
Lemon juice
1 teaspoon all-purpose flour

Cream butter and sugar. Blend in almond extract and egg. Stir in macaroon crumbs.

Plunge peaches into boiling water for about 20 seconds to loosen skins. Peel quickly and drop into cold water containing about 1 tablespoon of lemon juice.

Halve peaches and remove pits. Slice each half into 3 or 4 slices into a buttered 1½-quart baking dish. Sprinkle with flour. Spread macaroon mixture on top.

Bake in 350°F. oven 50 to 60 minutes until top is lightly browned.

To serve hot: Cover baking dish with foil and overwrap in several layers of newspaper and a heavy towel or transport foil-wrapped dish in insulated carrier.

To serve cold: Let dessert stand 1 hour after it is out of the oven. Cover baking dish and chill in the refrigerator. Carry to picnic in insulated cooler.

Makes 6 servings

GREEK TAVERNA SUPPER

Cucumber Dip
Lamb Chops á la Greque
Bean and Lentil Salad   Tomatoes
Honey Spice Cake   Grapes
Ouzo   White Wine
Coffee

Informality reigns at this picnic with laughter and pleasant conversation as much a part of the menu as the food. If there is a musical instrument handy, let it be played so everyone can sing along.

Cucumber Dip

2 medium cucumbers, peeled,
    seeded, and finely chopped
2 cloves garlic, minced
1 cup plain yogurt
1 teaspoon vinegar
2 teaspoons dill weed
Salt
Celery, zucchini, or other raw
    vegetable dippers

Combine cucumber, garlic, yogurt, vinegar, and dill weed. Add salt to taste. Chill at least 1 hour to blend flavors. Carry to picnic with other cold foods.

Wash and cut up vegetable dippers. Pack in plastic bag and carry to picnic in cooler.
Makes 6 servings

Lamb Chops á la Greque

6 lamb shoulder chops, cut at
    least 1 inch thick
2 cloves garlic
Dried oregano
Salt
Pepper
¼ cup olive oil
¼ cup lemon juice

Cut 6 rectangles of heavy-duty foil, each measuring about 3 times the width of a lamb chop one way and 1½ times the other. Place a chop in center of each piece of foil.

Cut each garlic clove crosswise into 6 slices. Make two slits in each chop and insert a slice of garlic. Sprinkle each chop with ¼ teaspoon crushed oregano, ¼ teaspoon salt, and several dashes pepper.

Blend oil and lemon juice with a small whisk. Divide mixture among chops.

Bring long ends of foil together and fold down toward meat, leaving a little head space for steam during cooking. Fold up shorter ends of foil to complete packet. Arrange packets in a shallow baking or roasting pan. Bake in 350°F. oven 1½ hours.

Wrap pan in several layers of newspaper and cover with a heavy towel. Or transfer packets to insulated carrier, being careful not to puncture foil. For maximum eating enjoyment, serve within 2 hours.
Makes 6 servings

Bean and Lentil Salad

1 cup lentils
2½ cups water
¾ teaspoon salt
1 cup chopped carrots
1 cup chopped celery
2 cups cooked green beans
½ cup bottled Italian salad
    dressing

Rinse lentils in cold running water. Bring lentils, water, and salt to a boil in a 2-quart saucepan. Reduce heat and simmer, covered, 15 to 20 minutes or until lentils are just barely tender. Stir occasionally.

Add carrots, celery, and another ¼ cup water, if necessary. Continue simmering about 5 minutes until vegetables are crisp-tender. Drain mixture if all cooking liquid has not been absorbed.

Transfer lentil mixture to salad bowl; toss with green beans. Toss with bottled Italian salad dressing. Chill. Carry to picnic in insulated cooler.

Makes 6 servings

Honey Spice Cake

½ cup butter or margarine
1 cup sugar
2 eggs
½ teaspoon grated orange peel

¼ cup orange juice
1 teaspoon vanilla
2 cups all-purpose flour
1 teaspoon baking powder
½ teaspoon baking soda
½ teaspoon salt
½ teaspoon ground cinnamon
½ teaspoon ground nutmeg
½ teaspoon ground mace
¼ teaspoon ground cloves
½ cup sour cream
⅓ cup honey
⅓ cup sugar
¼ teaspoon ground cinnamon
½ cup water

Cream butter and sugar until light and fluffy. Add eggs one at a time, beating well after each addition. Add orange peel, orange juice, and vanilla.

Stir together flour, baking powder, soda, salt, cinnamon, nutmeg, mace, and cloves. Add alternately to creamed mixture with sour cream, beginning and ending with flour mixture.

Turn into a greased and floured 9-inch-square pan. Bake in 350°F. oven 20 to 25 minutes.

Meanwhile make honey syrup by combining honey, sugar, cinnamon, and water in a 1-quart saucepan. (Do not use a smaller pan as mixture boils up quickly.) Stir until sugar dissolves. Bring mixture to a boil and cook over medium heat, stirring occasionally, for 15 minutes.

Spoon syrup over cake while cake is still warm. Start at center and work out to edges of the cake. When cake is cool, cut into squares.

Makes 9 squares

SULTAN'S TRAY

Persian or Casaba Melon
Marinated Lamb
Tabouleh
Honey-Nut Strips or Baklava
Red Wine   Coffee

Locate a large brass tray or polish enough small ones to hold the various dishes of food. Although an authentic Turkish fabric for the tablecloth may be difficult to come by, an attic or thrift shop might yield a printed shawl or piece of drapery that will suit the purpose.

Marinated Lamb

3 to 4 pounds leg of lamb
    (sirloin half)
½ cup cooking oil
⅓ cup lemon juice
½ cup finely chopped onion
1 teaspoon salt
¼ teaspoon coarsely ground
    pepper
2 tablespoons snipped parsley

Place leg of lamb in a large plastic bag. Combine oil, lemon juice, onion, salt, pepper, and parsley and pour over meat. Close top of bag. *Note*: standing the bag in a deep bowl keeps more of the meat surface covered with the marinade.

Refrigerate meat 4 to 6 hours, turning bag occasionally. Lift lamb out of marinade. Save marinade to use as a basting sauce for the meat.

Place lamb on a rack in an open pan. Insert a roast-meat thermometer in the center of the thickest muscle. Roast, uncovered, in a 325°F. oven until meat thermometer registers 135°F. for rare (about 1 hour), 150°F. for medium (about 1 hour and 15 minutes), or 160°F. for well done (about 1 hour and 30 minutes).

Baste meat occasionally during roasting time with reserved marinade.

To serve hot: Remove roast-meat thermometer. Immediately set roast on heavy-duty foil and wrap securely. Carry to picnic in an insulated container. Rare is difficult to maintain if the meat is not served within an hour of packing. Medium and well done are quite satisfactory if held 2 hours, depending on the efficiency of the insulated carrier. Carve at serving time.

To serve cold: Let roast stand about 20 minutes before carving into thin slices across the grain of the meat. Arrange slices in a single layer in a shallow foil-lined pan. Refrigerate until meat is cold. Stack slices with layers of waxed paper or plastic wrap in between. Wrap in foil. Chill until time to leave. Transfer package to insulated cooler.

Makes 8 servings

Picnic pointer: Suggested roasting times and internal temperatures are based on the fact that meat continues to cook after it comes out of the oven. This is particularly important if you plan to wrap the meat and carry it hot to the picnic.

Tabouleh

2 cups boiling water
1 cup dry bulgur wheat
1 cucumber, peeled, seeded,
    and coarsely chopped
2 tomatoes, peeled, seeded, and
    chopped
1 small zucchini, chopped
¼ cup sliced green onions with
    tops
2 tablespoons fresh mint leaves
    or 1 teaspoon dried mint
    leaves, crushed
2 tablespoons snipped parsley
¼ cup olive oil
¼ cup cooking oil
½ cup lemon juice
1 teaspoon salt

Pour boiling water over bulgur, cover, and let stand at least 2 hours.

Toss cucumber, tomatoes, zucchini, green onion, mint, and parsley with bulgur.

In screw-top jar combine oils, lemon juice, and salt. Pour over salad, tossing to coat. Cover. Chill several hours or overnight. Carry to picnic in insulated cooler.

At serving time toss mixture again to bring up dressing that has collected at bottom of bowl.

Makes 6 servings

Honey-Nut Strips

¾ cup butter or margarine
1 cup sugar
¼ cup honey
1 egg
¼ teaspoon almond extract
2¼ cups all-purpose flour
1½ teaspoons baking soda
½ teaspoon salt
¼ teaspoon ground cinnamon
¼ teaspoon ground nutmeg
6 tablespoons finely chopped
    almonds

Cream butter and sugar. Add honey, egg, and almond extract. Mix well.

Stir together flour, soda, salt, cinnamon, and nutmeg. Add to creamed mixture and beat well.

Divide dough into 6 parts. Shape each into a 12-inch roll and place 2 of them 3 inches apart on a greased 15-by-10-by-1-inch jelly-roll pan. Sprinkle 1 tablespoon of finely chopped almonds along top of each roll. Repeat with remaining rolls of dough.

Bake in 350°F. oven about 15 minutes or until light golden brown. Let cool in pan about 5 minutes. Cut in 1-inch diagonal strips. Remove strips to a rack to finish cooling. Store in a tightly covered container.

Makes 5 dozen cookies

ORIENTAL MEDLEY

Bean Sprout Salad
Five-Spice Chicken
Melon and Mandarin Bowl
Fortune Cookies
White Wine   Iced Tea

Americans' love affair with foods from the Orient has come a long way from the first encounter with soy sauce. Mandarin orange segments are almost a staple, and it is not unusual to find fresh bean sprouts in a supermarket. A trip to an Oriental grocery store may be necessary, however, to find the five-spice powder and canned lychees that set this menu apart.

Bean Sprout Salad

1 pound fresh bean sprouts
1 cup thinly sliced celery
1 9-ounce package frozen peas
Lettuce leaves
¾ cup mayonnaise
2 tablespoons soy sauce
2 teaspoons lemon juice
1½ teaspoons curry powder
¼ cup thinly sliced green onion

Wash bean sprouts and drain well. Pinch off any brown ends. Toss with celery.

Rinse frozen peas with boiling water and drain well. Toss with bean sprouts and celery. Refrigerate in covered container and carry to picnic in cooler.

Place washed and drained lettuce in plastic bag containing a crumpled paper towel. Carry to picnic with cold foods.

Combine mayonnaise, soy sauce, lemon juice, and curry powder. Stir in green onion. Chill. Carry to picnic in insulated cooler. Toss with bean sprout mixture just before serving. Mound on lettuce leaves.

Makes 6 servings

Five-Spice Chicken

2 2½- to 3-pound broiler-fryer
    chickens, cut up
½ cup soy sauce
½ cup cooking oil
2 tablespoons dry sherry or
    white wine
1 large clove garlic, finely
    minced
1 teaspoon salt
1 teaspoon grated fresh ginger
    root
2 teaspoons five-spice powder
    or 1 teaspoon ground
    cinnamon, 1 teaspoon
    crushed aniseed,
    ⅛ teaspoon ground
    nutmeg, ⅛ teaspoon
    ground cloves, and ⅛
    teaspoon pepper

Place drumsticks, thighs, and split breasts in a large plastic bag. (Freeze backs and wings for another use.) Stand bag in a deep bowl for stability.

Combine soy sauce, cooking oil, sherry, garlic, salt, ginger root, and five-spice powder. Pour over chicken. Close top of bag. Marinate chicken pieces 2 hours in the refrigerator, turning bag once or twice.

Drain chicken, reserving the marinade. Arrange pieces skin side up in a shallow roasting pan. Brush chicken surfaces with some of marinade. Roast, uncovered, in 350°F. oven about 1 hour or until brown and crisp. Brush chicken pieces with marinade every 20 minutes during roasting time.

To serve hot: Cover roasting pan with heavy-duty foil and wrap with several layers of newspaper and a large towel. Or place foil-wrapped pan in insulated carrier.

To serve cold: Let chicken stand in pan no more than 20 minutes before slipping pan into refrigerator to chill the chicken. When chicken is cold, transfer to covered container or wrap in foil. Carry to picnic in an insulated cooler.
Makes 6 servings

Melon and Mandarin Bowl

1 20-ounce can lychees
1 11-ounce can mandarin
    orange sections
2 or 3 cups watermelon balls

Drain lychees, reserving ½ cup syrup. Drain mandarin orange sections. Toss together lychees, orange sections, and melon balls. Pour reserved lychee syrup over the fruit. Chill in covered container. Carry to picnic in an insulated cooler or in a prechilled vacuum jug.
Makes 6 servings

MEXICAN FIESTA

Peppy Bean Dip
Corn Chips   Jicama
Orange-Basted Pork
Red, White, and Green Salad
Fresh Fruit   Polvorones
Margaritas or Mexican Beer
Coffee

Choose red, white, or green for tablecloth and dishes and add a profusion of paper streamers and flowers as decorations. Piñatas are traditional at Christmastime but are often available in Mexican shops year-round. If you can locate one, fill it with hard candies and have guests swat at it with a stick while blindfolded. Once it is opened, everyone shares in the treats.

Peppy Bean Dip

1 15-ounce can refried beans
1 cup sour cream
2 tablespoons chopped green
     chilies, rinsed and drained
Few drops hot pepper sauce
     (optional)
Shredded Cheddar cheese
1 large jicama, peeled and
     cubed
Juice of ½ lime

Blend sour cream into beans. Stir in chilies. Season with hot pepper sauce, if desired. Pack dip in covered container. Chill. Carry to picnic in cooler. Pack cheese in plastic bag in cooler and use to garnish dip before serving.

Sprinkle jicama pieces with lime juice in container with tight-fitting lid. Carry to picnic in cooler and have frilly cocktail picks to use with jicama cubes as dippers.

Makes 6 to 8 servings

Orange-Basted Pork

2½ to 3 pounds boneless pork
    shoulder roast, rolled and
    tied
½ teaspoon grated orange peel
¼ cup orange juice
1 tablespoon cooking oil
½ teaspoon chili powder
¼ teaspoon salt

Place pork roast on a rack in a shallow roasting pan. Insert meat thermometer in center, making sure tip rests in muscle and not in seam of roast.

Combine orange peel, orange juice, oil, chili powder, and salt in a small bowl. Brush surface of roast with some of this mixture.

Roast in 325°F. oven about 2 hours or until meat thermometer registers 170°F. Baste roast with orange juice mixture at intervals during the roasting time. Let roast stand 1 hour. Wrap in foil and refrigerate. Carry to picnic in insulated cooler.

Makes 6 to 8 servings

Red, White, and Green Salad

Incorporating the colors of the Mexican flag in foods served is popular south of the border. This is an arranged salad in which each color is kept separate.

1 small head cauliflower,
     broken into flowerets
2 very ripe avocados
2 tablespoons chopped onion
2 tablespoons lemon juice
1 small clove garlic, minced
¾ teaspoon salt
¼ teaspoon pepper
3 to 4 tomatoes
Thinly sliced green onions with
     tops
Cilantro or parsley
Lettuce (optional)

The white: Cook cauliflower until just tender in a covered saucepan in a small amount of boiling salted water. Total cooking time will be 5 to 15 minutes, depending on the size of the pieces. Do not overcook. Drain and chill in covered container in refrigerator.

The green: Peel and pit avocados. Cut up into blender container. Add onion, lemon juice, garlic, salt, and pepper. Process until smooth. Store in refrigerator in tightly covered container. Pack in insulated cooler.

The red: Pack tomatoes in insulated cooler along with green onions, cilantro, and lettuce.

Place avocado mixture in a small bowl in center of small round platter. Mound cauliflower in a circle around bowl. Arrange sliced tomatoes on outside of platter. Sprinkle sliced onions and snipped cilantro or parsley over top of vegetables. (Lettuce may be used to line plate, if desired.)

Makes 6 to 8 servings

Polvorones *(Mexican Wedding Cakes)*

1 cup butter or margarine
½ cup sifted powdered sugar
1 teaspoon vanilla
2 cups all-purpose flour
¾ cup finely chopped pecans
⅛ teaspoon salt
Powdered sugar

Cream butter, sugar, and vanilla. Stir together flour, pecans, and salt. Work dry ingredients into creamed mixture. Dough will be stiff.

Roll dough into 1-inch balls and place on ungreased baking sheet. Bake in 350°F. oven about 15 minutes. Cookies should be set but only very lightly browned.

Roll warm cookies in powdered sugar and cool on a rack. Roll in powdered sugar again when cool. Store in tightly covered container.

Makes 3 dozen cookies

CANADIAN FLING

Cheddar Cheese Soup
Boiled Beef Brisket
Garden Potato Salad
Relish Tray
Maple Tartlets
Red Wine
Coffee

The land of the maple leaf makes its own contributions to picnic fare. The Cheddar Cheese Soup is not like that made anywhere else and the maple-syrup desserts are world famous.

Cheddar Cheese Soup

2 tablespoons butter or
    margarine
¼ cup grated carrot
¼ cup finely chopped onion
¼ cup finely chopped celery
¼ cup shredded parsnip or
    turnip (optional but worth
    adding)
3 tablespoons all-purpose flour
1½ cups water
2 teaspoons beef bouillon
    granules
1 cup shredded Cheddar cheese
1½ cups milk
Salt and pepper

In heavy saucepan heat butter, carrot, onion, celery, and parsnip. When butter has melted, cover pan and reduce heat. Cook, stirring occasionally, about 5 minutes. Vegetables should be tender but not brown.

Stir in flour. Blend in water and beef bouillon granules. Cook over medium heat, stirring constantly until thickened and bubbly. Blend in cheese. Stir until melted.

Add milk. Continue cooking and stirring just until mixture comes to a boil. Immediately transfer to heated 1-quart vacuum bottle.

Makes 4 servings

Boiled Beef Brisket

1¾- to 2-pound piece fresh beef
    brisket
1 medium onion, sliced
1 bay leaf
1 teaspoon salt
⅛ teaspoon pepper

Trim excess fat from meat. Brown meat on all sides in heavy 4-quart saucepan. Lay onion slices and bay leaf over meat. Sprinkle with salt and pepper.

Add enough water to cover meat completely. Bring the liquid to a boil. Cover saucepan and reduce heat. Simmer meat about 2 hours or until fork-tender, adding water as needed to keep the meat submerged.

When meat is fork tender, remove bay leaf. Allow meat to cool 1 hour in the cooking liquid. (Shrinkage is reduced and meat is juicier if allowed to cool in liquid.)

Remove meat, wrap in foil, and refrigerate until ready to pack for picnic. Carry meat in an insulated cooler. Slice across the grain just before serving.

Makes 4 servings

Garden Potato Salad

3 medium potatoes
1 teaspoon sugar
1 teaspoon salt
1 teaspoon vinegar
¼ cup thinly sliced radish
¼ cup thinly sliced green onion
     with tops
¾ cup mayonnaise or salad
     dressing
2 hard-cooked eggs, coarsely
     chopped
1 tablespoon snipped parsley

In covered saucepan cook whole potatoes in their jackets in boiling salted water, until tender, about 25 minutes. Drain well.

Peel potatoes while still warm. Quarter and slice potatoes into a mixing bowl. Sprinkle and toss with sugar, salt, and vinegar. Add sliced radish and green onion.

Fold mayonnaise or salad dressing into potatoes. Carefully fold in eggs. Sprinkle parsley over salad. Cover and chill thoroughly. Carry to picnic in cooler.

Makes 4 servings

Maple Tartlets

An easy recipe to double for indoor party giving at other times of the year.

1 tablespoon butter or
     margarine
1 tablespoon flour
1 beaten egg
½ cup maple syrup
2 tablespoons water
¾ cup all-purpose flour

½ teaspoon salt
¼ cup shortening
Cold milk
¼ cup chopped walnuts

Melt butter in top of double boiler over hot water. Stir in 1 tablespoon flour. Combine egg, maple syrup, and water. Blend into butter-flour mixture. Cook, stirring constantly, until mixture is thickened and will mound slightly, about 10 minutes. Remove pan from hot water. Cool.

Stir together flour and salt for pastry. Cut shortening into flour with pastry blender or two knives. Mixture should contain pieces the size of small peas.

Sprinkle milk, 1 tablespoon at a time, over flour. Toss flour mixture with a fork after each tablespoon of milk. After 2 tablespoons of milk have been used, try to gather dough together. If it doesn't hold a ball, sprinkle another tablespoon of milk over crumbly mixture and try again. When dough can be compressed into a ball, let it rest 10 minutes.

Roll dough out ⅛ inch thick on lightly floured surface or pastry cloth. Cut 3-inch circles. Fit pastry circles into miniature muffin pans. Prick pastry with a fork. Bake at 425°F. for 5 or 6 minutes until lightly browned. Watch carefully so tarts do not get too dark. Cool tarts in pan.

Spoon filling into tarts. Sprinkle with chopped walnuts. Cover lightly with foil. Chill if not packing for picnic immediately. Carry to picnic in pan and pack with cold foods.
Makes 12 tartlets

Dates to Remember

Family Reunion
Patriots' Celebration
Packed-up Luau
Birthday Party Picnic
Tailgaters' Fan Fare

4

Occasional Outings

A phone call to say, "Let's get together for a picnic on the Fourth of July, or your birthday, or before the big game," makes a definite date for celebrating a friendship with happy conversation and plenty of good food. Likewise, actually reserving a park shelter and contacting all the relatives sets the wheels in motion for a family reunion.

Just because there is no holiday or big family doings in the offing, you do not have to go picnicless for any length of time. Simply choose an open date on the calendar, consult the weather bureau, and call a picnic to mark the occasion. A theme outing such as a luau works well in these circumstances because it isn't linked with a specific day or season and yet radiates the necessary festive feeling.

FAMILY REUNION

Cranberry Cooler
Breast of Turkey
Barley–Brown Rice Casserole
Broccoli-Cauliflower Salad
Corn Relish
Sliced Tomatoes
Buttered Hard Rolls
Chocolate Picnic Cake
Coffee   Colas

Cranberry Cooler

Give guests a choice of wine or fizzy version. Supplies provide 12 servings.

2 32-ounce bottles cranberry
    juice cocktail, chilled
2 bottles rosé wine (750 ml
    each), chilled
1 32-ounce bottle sparkling
    water, chilled
Ice cubes

Wine version: Put one or two ice cubes in glass and fill half with cranberry cocktail and half with rosé.

Fizzy version: Put one or two ice cubes in glass and fill half with cranberry cocktail and half with sparkling water.

Picnic Pointer: Transport chilled cranberry cocktail in vacuum jug with spigot. Carry wine and sparkling water to picnic in an ice chest.

Breast of Turkey

6- to 8-pound frozen turkey
    breast
Melted butter

Place turkey breast, skin side up, on a rack in a shallow pan. Brush skin with melted butter. Roast in 325°F. oven for 2¼ to 3¾ hours, depending on whether breast is thawed or frozen.

Note: Turkey breast may be cooked either directly from freezer or thawed before roasting. Frozen, it requires 3¼ to 3¾ hours in the oven. Thawing reduces roasting time about 1 hour. Thaw frozen turkey breast in opened bag in the refrigerator 1 or 2 days. You can shorten thawing time by placing unopened bag in cool water 4 to 8 hours. Change water frequently. Often it will be less bother to skip the thawing step and start roasting while breast is still frozen.

A roast-meat thermometer is the most accurate method of judging doneness. If the breast was thawed before roasting, the thermometer can be inserted before the turkey goes into the oven. Wait at least an hour before placing thermometer in frozen breast. In either case it is placed in the meat, not touching bone. An internal temperature of 170°F. indicates the end of roasting time.

Check roasting progress from time to time. You may need to shield the skin with a piece of lightweight foil to prevent over-browning.

To serve hot: Transfer cooked turkey breast to a large sheet of heavy-duty foil and wrap tightly. Overwrap in several layers of newspaper and cover with a heavy towel or small blanket such as a car robe. Better yet, carry wrapped turkey breast to picnic in an insulated container. Carve just before serving.

To serve cold: Let cooked turkey breast stand 1 hour. Wrap in foil and chill in refrigerator. Carry to picnic in an insulated cooler. Carve at serving time.

Makes 12 servings

Turkey for a Crowd

If the number of people increases, you may want to switch to roasting a whole bird rather than doing two breasts. If so, there are some special techniques for handling turkey as a picnic food.

Allow 1 pound of turkey per person when making your purchase. The 20-pound-and-over birds are often specially priced during summer months. It may be worthwhile to roast a big one and freeze what you don't take to the picnic. Thaw and roast the bird without stuffing, following directions and timings on turkey wrapper.

Don't take the carcass to the picnic. Besides being bulky and difficult to transport, you have to carry it home again and leftover meat still attached will have been out of refrigeration too long for safe eating.

After turkey is in the oven, scrub the cutting board or work surface used in getting it ready for roasting. One of the chief problems with food-related illness occurs because cooked poultry is carved on a board that was only wiped off after its last use. The cooked bird picked up the bacteria it left behind before cooking. Hot sudsy water, even a mild bleach solution, and a scalding rinse would have eliminated the problem.

Let turkey stand 1 hour after it comes from the oven. Line several baking sheets or shallow pans with heavy-duty foil. Place turkey on scrubbed board and carve. Spread turkey slices in pans so that meat is only 1 or 2 layers deep. As one pan is finished, cover lightly and place it in refrigerator before starting on the next pan. When all the turkey is thoroughly chilled, consolidate slices into several convenient-sized packages. Keep refrigerated until ready to pack for picnic. Carry in insulated cooler.

Barley–Brown Rice Casserole

¾ cup quick-cooking barley
¾ cup brown rice
½ cup butter or margarine
1 large onion, chopped
1 cup thinly sliced celery
2 4-ounce cans sliced
      mushroom stems and
      pieces
2 teaspoons dried sage, crushed
1 teaspoon salt
¼ teaspoon pepper
4 cups chicken broth

In skillet heat barley, brown rice, and onion in butter until onion is transparent but not brown. Add celery, mushrooms with liquid, sage, salt, and pepper. Transfer mixture to 2½- or 3-quart baking dish.

Set baking dish in 350°F. oven. Pour chicken broth over barley mixture. Stir gently. *Note*: If it looks like baking dish will be too full if all the broth is added at the beginning, add 3 cups of broth and stir in remaining 1 cup after some of the liquid has been absorbed.

Bake, covered, for 60 minutes, or until most of the liquid has been absorbed. Stir once or twice after the first 30 minutes.

Wrap hot casserole in several layers of newspaper and cover with a heavy towel. Or, carry to picnic in insulated container. Fluff with a fork before serving.

Makes 12 servings

Broccoli-Cauliflower Salad

4 cups raw broccoli pieces
4 cups raw cauliflower
    flowerets
1 small red onion, thinly sliced
1 cup cooking oil
¼ cup vinegar
¼ cup lemon juice
1 clove garlic, minced
2 teaspoons sugar
1 teaspoon salt
1 tablespoon fresh basil or 1½
    teaspoons dried basil

In 2¼-quart bowl toss broccoli, cauliflower, and red onion.

Place oil, vinegar, lemon juice, garlic, sugar, salt, and basil in blender container. Process until well combined. Pour over vegetables. Cover and marinate in refrigerator several hours. Retoss vegetables occasionally, spooning dressing up from bottom of bowl. Carry to picnic in cooler.

Makes 12 servings

Chocolate Picnic Cake

1¼ cups boiling water
3 1-ounce squares unsweetened
    chocolate, cut up
1 cup quick-cooking rolled oats
½ cup cooking oil
1 teaspoon vanilla
3 eggs
1½ cups all-purpose flour
1 teaspoon baking soda
½ teaspoon ground cinnamon
¾ cup granulated sugar
¾ cup packed brown sugar
½ cup chopped walnuts
½ cup semisweet chocolate
    pieces

Pour boiling water over chocolate and rolled oats in mixing bowl. Stir until chocolate is melted. Stir in oil and vanilla. Add eggs one at a time, beating well after each addition.

Stir together flour, baking soda, and cinnamon. Stir in sugars. Add to chocolate mixture and beat well.

Pour batter into greased 13-by-9-by-2-inch baking pan. Sprinkle nuts and chocolate pieces evenly over surface of cake. Bake in 350°F. oven 35 to 40 minutes or until cake tests done with a wooden pick. Cover pan when cake is cool.

Makes 12 servings

PATRIOTS' CELEBRATION

Clam Dip
Potato Chips   Celery Sticks
Ham
Rum-Pot Baked Beans
24-Hour Salad
Buttered Sourdough Bread
Watermelon Bowl
Beer
Soft Drinks

Clam Dip

1 8-ounce package cream
  cheese, cut into cubes and
  softened
2 tablespoons grated onion
2 tablespoons catsup
1 tablespoon lemon juice
2 teaspoons Worcestershire
  sauce
2 teaspoons prepared
  horseradish
Several dashes cayenne
1 6½-ounce can minced clams

Beat together cream cheese, grated onion, catsup, lemon juice, Worcestershire sauce, horseradish, and cayenne.

Drain clams, reserving liquid. Blend clams into cream cheese mixture. Add enough of clam liquid to make desired dipping consistency. Chill. Carry to picnic with cold foods.
Makes about 1½ cups

Ham

Several boneless ham styles await the shopper. All are fully cooked and may be carved right out of the picnic cooler. Plan on 5 servings per pound and keep the meat—even canned ham—in the refrigerator or cooler until serving time.

Rum-Pot Baked Beans

2 pounds dry pea beans or navy
    beans
4 quarts water
4 ounces salt pork, cut up
1 large onion, coarsely chopped
1 cup molasses
2 teaspoons dry mustard
1 teaspoon salt
¼ teaspoon pepper
½ cup rum

Rinse beans. In a large saucepan bring beans and water to a boil. Reduce heat and simmer 2 minutes. Remove pan from heat. Cover and let stand 1 hour. (Alternative method is to let beans soak overnight.)

Bring beans to a boil, reduce heat and simmer, uncovered, about 1 hour or until beans are tender. Drain beans, reserving cooking liquid.

Transfer beans to a 2½- to 3-quart casserole or bean pot. Stir in salt pork and onion. Combine 1 cup of reserved liquid with molasses, mustard, salt, and pepper. Pour over beans. Stir in enough additional reserved liquid to almost cover beans.

Bake in 300°F. oven 3½ to 4 hours. After beans have cooked 3½ hours, uncover and stir in rum. Continue cooking until mixture has desired juiciness.

Wrap hot covered casserole in several layers of newspaper and overwrap with heavy towel. Or carry covered casserole to picnic in an insulated carrier.
Makes 12 servings

24-Hour Salad

2 cups frozen peas, thawed
1 large cucumber, peeled,
    halved lengthwise, seeded,
    and thinly sliced
1 cup shredded Cheddar cheese
4 hard-cooked eggs, sliced
1 pint cottage cheese
¼ cup mayonnaise
½ teaspoon salt
1 tablespoon chopped onion
6 cups torn leaf lettuce
Salt and pepper
Chopped chives

Prepare vegetables, cheese, and eggs as directed.

Place cottage cheese, mayonnaise, salt, and chopped onion in blender container. Process just long enough to combine.

Place half the lettuce in the bottom of a large bowl. Sprinkle with half the cheese. Layer peas and then sliced egg. Sprinkle generously with salt and pepper.

Spread remaining lettuce over eggs. Top with cucumber and remaining shredded cheese. Spread cottage cheese dressing carefully over the top. Be sure it comes all the way to the edge to seal the bowl. Garnish with chives. Chill in refrigerator 24 hours or overnight.

Carry to picnic in an insulated cooler. Toss just before serving.
Makes 10 to 12 servings

Watermelon Bowl

1 whole watermelon
Cantaloupe balls or cubes,
    chilled
Cubed fresh pineapple, chilled
Blueberries, chilled
Fresh mint sprigs (optional)

Cut a thin slice off bottom of watermelon so it will sit firmly on platter or cutting board. Cut a larger slice off the top so that red flesh is exposed

Scoop out melon, making balls or cubes. Chill watermelon balls with the rest of the fruit. Carry to picnic in insulated cooler.

Using the edge of a cup for a pattern or drawing a sawtooth design with a ruler, cut rim of bowl in decorative fashion. Pack bowl, cut side down, in ice chest. At serving time pile chilled fruits in melon bowl. Garnish with sprigs of fresh mint.
Makes 10 to 12 servings

PACKED-UP LUAU

Salmon Spread   Sesame Crackers
Ham Wikiwiki
Pineapple-Papaya Salad
Hard Rolls   Butter
Coconut Pound Cake
Mai Tais   Coffee

Salmon Spread

1 8-ounce can salmon
1 3-ounce package cream
    cheese, softened
2 teaspoons lemon juice
1 teaspoon grated onion
½ teaspoon prepared
    horseradish

Drain salmon. Remove any bones or skin. Add salmon to remaining ingredients and beat until well combined. Pack in container with a cover. Chill. Carry to picnic with cold foods.
Makes about 1½ cups

Ham Wikiwiki

Translated, this means hurry-up ham.

4 tablespoons guava jelly
Juice of 1 lime
½ teaspoon dry mustard
2 pounds boneless ham steak

Melt jelly in a large skillet. Blend in lime juice and mustard. Cut ham into 8 serving-sized portions. Add to jelly mixture and simmer gently, spooning sauce over meat and turning meat once or twice until well glazed.

To serve hot: Continue heating until ham is well heated through. Wrap in foil and carry ham to picnic in insulated carrier.

To serve cold: Transfer ham to covered container. Chill. Carry to picnic in insulated cooler.

Makes 8 servings

Pineapple-Papaya Salad

Fresh pineapple chunks or 16-
    ounce can juice-packed
    pineapple chunks, drained
2 ripe papayas, peeled, seeded,
    and cubed
8 large lettuce leaves
1 cup French dressing

Gently toss pineapple chunks and papaya cubes. Chill. Carry to picnic in covered bowl in cooler. Wash lettuce and drain. Carry to picnic in plastic bag with crumpled paper towel in the bottom. Pack with cold foods.

At serving time place lettuce leaf on each plate. Spoon some of fruit mixture onto lettuce and drizzle each salad with about 1 tablespoon of French dressing.

Makes 8 servings

Coconut Pound Cake

1 cup butter or margarine
1 cup sugar
4 eggs
1 teaspoon almond extract
½ teaspoon vanilla
¼ teaspoon salt
1 cup flaked coconut
2 cups all-purpose flour

(For maximum volume in this delicate pound cake, let butter and eggs come to room temperature before mixing.)

In mixer bowl cream butter until fluffy. Add sugar slowly and continue creaming for 6 minutes, scraping sides of bowl from time to time.

Add eggs one at a time, beating well after each addition. Add almond extract, vanilla, and salt. Fold in coconut.

Gradually add flour, mixing just until blended. Turn mixture into a greased and floured 9-by-5-by-3-inch loaf pan. Place oven racks so that cake will be in the center of the oven.

Preheat oven to 325°F. Bake cake 50 to 60 minutes. Cool in pan 10 minutes. Remove from pan and finish cooling on a rack. Wrap in foil. Slice at picnic.

Makes 1 loaf; 10 to 12 slices

BIRTHDAY PARTY PICNIC

Celebration Punch
Roast Beef Rolls
Potato Salad Indienne
Garden Vegetable Platter
Birthday Angel Food Cake
Vanilla Ice Cream or Whipped Cream Cheese
Fresh Blueberry Sauce
Iced Tea

Celebration Punch

1 24-ounce bottle white grape
    juice, chilled
1 bottle dry white wine (750
    ml), chilled
1 32-ounce bottle sparkling
    water, chilled
Ice cubes

Pour half of grape juice and half of white wine over ice cubes in a 2-quart pitcher. Fill pitcher with sparkling water. Refill pitcher with remaining ingredients.
Makes 16 servings

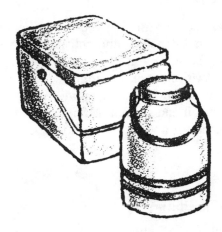

Picnic pointers: Serving punch on a picnic taxes the ingenuity. No one wants to transport an heirloom glass punch bowl and the manufacturers of vacuum jugs don't recommend carrying carbonated beverages in them because the gas can weaken the seal on the jug.

For large groups: If you prefer not to rent a punch bowl, look around the kitchen for a large container to disguise. For example, make a drawstring apron to tie around a 6- to 8-quart kettle. The fabric should complement the tablecloth or party theme. Depending on the type of handles on the kettle, you may have to cut slits in the fabric to fit around them. Fasten bows or flowers on the handles.

For small groups: A 2-quart pitcher is an easy substitute for a punch bowl. Often you can find one reasonably priced at discount or variety stores. Garage sales are another likely source.

Since this is a birthday party, try wrapping washed ½-gallon milk cartons with oilcloth or other waterproof material to look like a present. At the picnic open the tops and mix the punch in the carton. Don't fill too full and you will be able to pour or ladle the punch quite easily.

Roast Beef Rolls

Buy sliced roast beef at the deli counter, allowing one slice per roll. Have the deli cut one slice and roll it up so you can see what it looks like. Use the sample as a guide for determining whether to plan on one or two rolls per serving.

At home roll each slice into a cigar-shaped cylinder. Wrap completed rolls in foil and store in refrigerator. Carry to picnic in an insulated cooler. For a variation, roll the beef around a slender dill pickle strip.

Garden Vegetable Platter

Pack an assortment of sliced tomatoes, raw cauliflower flowerets, cucumber or zucchini cut into chunks, green onions, and other vegetables in season when the picnic is planned. Transport vegetables in covered containers or plastic bags tucked in with the cold foods. Add olives or pickles to suit your fancy.

Potato Salad Indienne

8 medium potatoes
2 tablespoons cooking oil
1 teaspoon ground turmeric
½ teaspoon dry mustard
1 teaspoon salt
2 large onions, chopped

Boil potatoes in their jackets in enough boiling salted water to cover until potatoes are just tender. Do not overcook. Peel potatoes and cut into 1-inch cubes.

In large heavy skillet heat oil, turmeric, mustard, and salt. Add chopped onions and cook until tender. Add potatoes and toss with onion mixture until well coated.

To serve cold: Refrigerate mixture 8 hours or overnight. Carry to picnic in ice chest or cooler.

To serve hot: Cover skillet and continue heating and stirring occasionally until mixture is piping hot. Wrap skillet in several layers of newspaper and heavy towels or transfer contents to a covered bowl and carry to picnic in an insulated container.

Makes 8 servings

Birthday Cake

Let a bake shop take care of the cake. If you have a penchant for decorated cakes, they are equipped to write Happy Birthday in almost any color or to inscribe a personal greeting. However, to some people an angel food cake says birthday and local bakeries often excel in this delicate, airy cake. Top wedges of angel food with a scoop of ice cream and Fresh Blueberry Sauce or a dollop of whipped cream cheese and Fresh Blueberry Sauce.

Vanilla Ice Cream

Picnic pointer: Ice cream must be packed with dry ice and plenty of insulation around it in order to stay firm enough to serve at a picnic. If you place the order far enough in advance, an ice cream specialty shop or distributor for a commercial ice cream plant in the area can tell you how to do it or provide the necessary equipment.

Whipped Cream Cheese

This fluffy topping provides an alternate to the ice cream and is delicious with angel food and Fresh Blueberry Sauce.

Purchase a container of whipped cream cheese or do it yourself by beating an 8-ounce package of cream cheese with a little milk until fluffy. Either type must be kept chilled until serving time.

Fresh Blueberry Sauce

¾ cup sugar
¼ cup water
1 teaspoon lemon juice
1 pint fresh blueberries
Several dashes ground
    cinnamon

In a saucepan bring sugar and water to a boil. Add lemon juice and blueberries. Simmer 2 minutes and remove from heat. Stir in cinnamon. Cool. Store in covered container in refrigerator. Carry to picnic with cold foods. Spoon over vanilla ice cream as a sundae or top ice cream or whipped cream cheese and angel food cake.
Makes about 2 cups

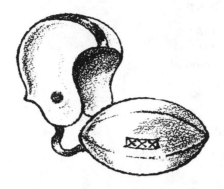

TAILGATERS' FAN FARE

Cheddar-Blue Spread
Crackers   Celery Sticks
Kielbasa-Beef Soup
Pumpernickel Bread
Pickles
Apple Pie Bars
Beer
Coffee

Cheddar-Blue Spread

1 8-ounce package cream cheese
1 cup shredded sharp Cheddar cheese
2 ounces crumbled blue cheese
1 to 2 tablespoons milk
½ teaspoon Worcestershire sauce

Let cheeses come to room temperature. Combine all ingredients in mixer, blender, or food processer until smooth. Pack in 2-cup container. Cover and chill. Carry to picnic in insulated cooler.
Makes 2 cups

Kielbasa-Beef Soup

1 tablespoon cooking oil
2 cloves garlic, minced
1 pound beef stew meat
1 28-ounce can tomatoes,
    chopped
4 cups water
1 cup strong coffee
2 tablespoons packed brown
    sugar
1 beef bouillon cube
1 teaspoon salt
½ teaspoon dried sage, crushed
½ teaspoon fennel seed
⅛ teaspoon pepper
4 carrots, sliced ¼ inch thick
1 cup sliced celery
1 large onion, sliced
12 ounces kielbasa (Polish
    sausage), sliced ¼ inch
    thick
1 10-ounce package frozen
    whole-kernel corn

Trim excess fat from beef and cut meat into ½-inch pieces. Heat
oil and garlic in 4-quart kettle. Brown stew meat. Add tomatoes,
water, coffee, brown sugar, bouillon cube, salt, sage, fennel seed,
and pepper. Bring to a boil. Cover pan and reduce heat. Simmer
1½ hours until meat is tender.

Add carrots, celery, onion, kielbasa, and corn. Bring to boil
again. Cover and reduce heat. Simmer about 10 minutes until
vegetables are crisp-tender. Taste broth. Add salt or pepper as
needed.

Transfer to 1-gallon heated wide-mouth vacuum jug. Serve
soup in mugs.
Makes about 10 cups

Apple Pie Bars

1 cup all-purpose flour
½ cup packed brown sugar
½ teaspoon salt
½ teaspoon baking soda
1 cup quick-cooking rolled oats
½ cup butter or margarine
¼ cup granulated sugar
1 teaspoon ground cinnamon
2½ cups cooking apples, peeled
    and thinly sliced
¼ cup powdered sugar
1 to 2 teaspoons milk

Stir together flour, brown sugar, salt, and soda. Stir in rolled oats.

Cut butter into oats mixture until crumbly. Pat half of mixture into greased 8-inch-square pan.

Combine granulated sugar and cinnamon. Toss with apple slices. Spread apples over mixture in pan. Top with remaining oat mixture.

Bake in 350°F. oven for 45 minutes. Cool. Blend 1 teaspoon milk into powdered sugar. Mixture will be thick. Add only enough additional milk to make a consistency for drizzling over bars. Cut into squares.
Makes 16 bars

Surprises du Jour

Gazpacho

Curried Avocado Soup

Garden Pea Potage

Sherried Chicken Broth

Salad Niçoise

Curried Orange–Chicken Salad

Tostada Salad

Italian Sweet Rusks

Oatmeal Crispies

Brandied Pear–Pecan Pie

Pineapple-Rhubarb Pie

5

Midday Repasts

Why settle for a mediocre take-along lunch when a bit of imagination and a small outlay for equipment can provide great food every day?

Three purchases make all this possible. The first is a wide-mouth vacuum bottle, the second a small insulated carrier, and the third a container of refreezable gel.

The vacuum bottle is for carrying hot or cold soups or mayonnaise and salad dressings for salads and sandwich fillings. Since these thermal containers are available in several sizes, you may want to have more than one.

The insulated lunch box or small carrier provides storage for perishables during the several-hour wait between breakfast and lunch. Thanks to new lightweight insulation materials and molded plastics, designs of these lunch boxes get better and more efficient with each season's production. Zip-up padded pouches are another handy option.

Containers of refreezable gel can be purchased at any sporting goods store. When not in use, store them in the freezer overnight, then pack them with the lunch in the morning. Take them home in the evening and put them back in the freezer.

Thus equipped, you are ready to make and enjoy any of the tasty soups and salads in this and other chapters. A few recipes for cookies and pies are included for a sweet ending to any repast.

SOUPS

Gazpacho

A refreshing soup and salad in each serving.

1½ cups tomato juice
1 tablespoon olive oil or cooking
    oil
1 tablespoon wine vinegar
1 small clove garlic, cut in half
1 medium tomato, peeled and
    quartered
4 ½-inch slices unpeeled
    cucumber
½ small green pepper,
    quartered
1 stalk celery, chopped
½ small onion
½ teaspoon salt
Few drops bottled hot pepper
    sauce

Place all ingredients in a blender container. Process only a few seconds until vegetables are coarsely chopped. Chill thoroughly.

Carry to picnic in chilled 1-quart vacuum bottle. Serve in mugs.
Makes 4 servings

Curried Avocado Soup

2 tablespoons butter or
     margarine
1 small onion, finely chopped
1 stalk celery, thinly sliced
1½ teaspoons curry powder
1 teaspoon salt
⅛ teaspoon pepper
⅛ teaspoon ground allspice
1½ tablespoons all-purpose
     flour
1½ cups chicken broth or 1½
     teaspoons chicken bouillon
     granules plus 1½ cups
     boiling water
1 very ripe avocado
1 tablespoon lemon juice
1 teaspoon prepared
     horseradish
1½ cups milk

Melt butter in 1-quart saucepan. Stir in onion, celery, curry powder, salt, pepper, and allspice. Cook, stirring occasionally, until vegetables are transparent but not brown.

Blend flour into butter and vegetables. Add chicken broth all at once. Cook over moderate heat, stirring constantly, until thickened and bubbly. Remove pan from heat.

Peel and cut up avocado into blender container. Add lemon juice, horseradish, and 1 or 2 tablespoons of soup mixture. Process a few seconds. Add remaining soup. Process just until mixture is smooth.

Return soup to saucepan. Stir in milk and cook, stirring constantly, until heated through. Do not let mixture boil.

To serve hot: Pour immediately into heated vacuum bottle.

To serve cold: Remove pan of soup from heat. Let stand 10 or 15 minutes. Pour into container with a lid. Refrigerate until very cold. Pour into chilled vacuum bottle.

Makes 4 servings

Garden Pea Potage

4 cups water
2 tablespoons chicken bouillon
    granules
2 carrots, coarsely chopped
2 stalks celery, coarsely
    chopped
1 medium potato, peeled and
    chopped
1 large onion, chopped
1 clove garlic, minced
1 teaspoon salt
½ teaspoon dried rosemary
2 cups frozen peas

In saucepan combine water, bouillon granules, carrots, celery, potato, onion, garlic, salt, and rosemary. Simmer, covered, until vegetables are very tender. Add peas and boil 1 minute.

Transfer mixture to blender container and process until puréed. Pour into covered container. Chill thoroughly. Carry to picnic in chilled vacuum bottle. Serve cold.
Makes 3 to 4 servings

Sherried Chicken Broth

3½ cups chicken broth
¼ cup dry sherry
4 lemon slices

Bring chicken broth to a rolling boil. Add sherry. Pour hot soup into heated vacuum bottle. Pack lemon slices in plastic container. Garnish each serving with lemon slice at serving time.
Makes 4 servings

SALADS

Salad Nicoise

A colorful main-dish salad from the French Riviera.

1 teaspoon Dijon mustard
¼ teaspoon salt
2 tablespoons wine vinegar
6 tablespoons oil (all olive oil or
    all cooking oil or half of
    each)
Freshly ground black pepper
4 cups torn lettuce
1 6½-ounce can chunk-style
    tuna
2 medium potatoes, cooked,
    peeled, and diced
2 medium tomatoes
2 hard-cooked eggs
1 16-ounce can green beans
Ripe olives for garnish

In small mixing bowl combine mustard and salt. Gradually stir in wine vinegar to make a smooth paste. Add oil, a little at a time, beating well with whisk or rotary beater after each addition. Season to taste with freshly ground black pepper. Transfer dressing to screw-top jar. Chill. Carry to picnic in insulated container.

Store washed lettuce in plastic bag with crumpled paper towel in bottom. Chill.

Chill tuna, potatoes, tomatoes, eggs, and olives several hours or overnight.

Pack dressing and individual chilled ingredients in an insulated cooler.

To assemble salads: Remove paper towel from plastic bag containing torn lettuce. Shake up dressing and toss about 2 tablespoons of it with torn lettuce. Divide lettuce among 4 salad plates.

Drain tuna and divide can into 4 portions. Place one portion in center of lettuce on each plate.

Arrange potatoes, tomato wedges, sliced egg, and drained green beans in mounds around the tuna, keeping each item separate. Drizzle some of the salad dressing over each mound. Garnish with sliced ripe olives.

Makes 4 servings

Picnic pointer: Don't forget the can opener when packing equipment. Or open cans at home and transfer chilled contents to small covered containers.

Curried Orange-Chicken Salad

½ cup mayonnaise
2 green onions, thinly sliced
¼ teaspoon curry powder
1 teaspoon grated orange peel
1 orange
2 cups cubed cooked chicken
2 cups frozen peas
½ cup thinly sliced celery
2 tablespoons finely chopped
    green pepper
Leaf lettuce
1 cup chow mein noodles

In a small bowl stir together mayonnaise, green onion, curry powder, and orange peel. Cover. Refrigerate. Carry to picnic in insulated cooler.

Peel and section orange. Chill and pack with cold foods.

Salt chicken cubes lightly. Refrigerate in covered container. Rinse peas with hot water. Drain well. Toss with chicken, celery, and green pepper. Cover and refrigerate. Carry to picnic with cold foods.

Wash lettuce and pat dry. Pack in plastic bag with crumpled paper towel in bottom. Keep chilled.

To assemble salads: At serving time divide lettuce among 4 salad plates. Drain orange sections, reserving juice. Toss oranges, chicken, peas, celery, and green pepper. Thin dressing if desired with a small amount of reserved orange juice. Fold dressing into salad. Add chow mein noodles and toss. Serve at once.
Makes 4 servings

Tostada Salad

1 pound ground beef
1 small onion, chopped
1 clove garlic, minced
1 teaspoon salt
¼ teaspoon chili powder
1 16-ounce can kidney beans,
    drained
1 large head lettuce
2 large tomatoes, coarsely
    chopped
1 cup shredded Cheddar cheese
¼ cup sliced ripe olives
1 8-ounce bottle creamy
    Russian salad dressing
Corn or tortilla chips

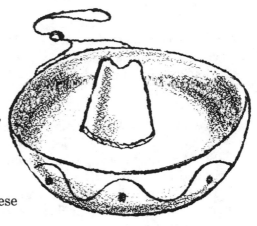

Partially cook ground beef. Drain off excess fat. Add chopped onion, garlic, salt, and chili powder. Continue cooking until onions are tender. Remove from heat. Stir in kidney beans. Transfer to covered bowl and refrigerate several hours. Carry to picnic in an insulated cooler or in wide-mouth vacuum bottle.

Core and wash lettuce. Drain well. Place lettuce in a plastic bag with a crumpled paper towel in the bottom. Carry to picnic with other cold foods.

To assemble salads: Tear up lettuce and divide among 6 plates. Spoon meat mixture over lettuce. Top with tomatoes, cheese, and olives. Pass Russian dressing. Serve with corn chips.
Makes 6 servings

DESSERTS

Italian Sweet Rusks

6 tablespoons butter or
    margarine
⅔ cup sugar
3 slightly beaten eggs
¼ teaspoon vanilla
½ teaspoon anise extract or ¼
    teaspoon almond extract
2 cups all-purpose flour
2 teaspoons baking powder
¼ teaspoon salt

Cream butter and sugar thoroughly. Add eggs, vanilla, and anise or almond extract. Beat well.

Stir together flour, baking powder, and salt. Add to creamed mixture and beat well.

Divide dough in half. On a greased baking sheet shape each portion into a loaf 10 inches long and 3 inches wide. Leave 2 inches between loaves.

Bake in 375°F. oven about 15 minutes until pale brown. Cool in pan about 5 minutes. Cut loaves into ¾-inch slices. Turn slices on sides and toast under broiler until lightly browned. Turn slices and toast on other sides. Store in loosely covered container.
Makes 2 dozen cookies

Oatmeal Crispies

½ cup shortening
½ cup packed brown sugar
½ cup granulated sugar
1 beaten egg
½ teaspoon vanilla
1 cup all-purpose flour
½ teaspoon salt

½ teaspoon baking soda
1½ cups quick-cooking rolled
    oats
¼ cup chopped nuts

Cream shortening and sugars. Add egg and vanilla and beat thoroughly.

Stir together flour, salt, soda, and rolled oats. Add to creamed mixture. Mix well. Stir in nuts.

Shape dough into 2 rolls each 2 inches in diameter. Chill several hours. Slice ⅛-inch thick and place on ungreased baking sheet. Bake in 375°F. oven 10 to 15 minutes until lightly browned. *Makes 3 dozen cookies*

Brandied Pear-Pecan Pie

Pastry for two-crust 8-inch pie
    (see recipe below)
4 cups ripe pear slices
1 tablespoon lemon juice
¼ cup all-purpose flour
½ cup chopped pecans
½ cup packed brown sugar
2 tablespoons butter
2 tablespoons brandy

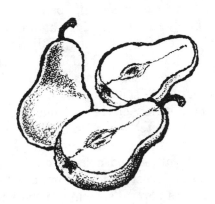

Toss pears with lemon juice and arrange fruit in pastry-lined pan. Sprinkle flour and pecans over pears.

In a small saucepan heat brown sugar, butter, and brandy, stirring until sugar dissolves. Pour over pears.

Adjust top crust over filling. Fold top crust under bottom crust and crimp edges around rim to seal. Cut several slits in top crust to allow steam to escape during baking. Protect edges of crust with 2-inch-wide strip of foil.

Bake in 425°F. oven 40 to 50 minutes or until crust is browned and filling begins to bubble up through slits. *Makes 6 servings*

Pastry for Two-Crust 8-inch Pie

1¾ cups all-purpose flour
¾ teaspoon salt
⅔ cup shortening
Cold milk

Stir together flour and salt. Cut shortening into flour with pastry blender or two knives. Mixture should contain pieces the size of small peas.

Sprinkle milk, 1 tablespoon at a time, over flour. Toss flour mixture with a fork after each tablespoon of milk. After 3 tablespoons of milk have been used, try to gather dough together. If it doesn't hold in a ball, sprinkle another tablespoon of milk over crumbly mixture and try again. Repeat if necessary. When dough can be compressed into a ball, let it rest 10 minutes.

Divide dough in half. Roll out one portion on a lightly floured surface or pastry cloth. Make a circle 1½ inches larger than the rim of an 8-inch pie pan.

Fold pastry circle into quarters and transfer to pie pan. Pat but do not stretch dough to fit pan. Add filling. Trim bottom crust to within 1 inch of rim of pie pan.

Roll out second crust the same as the first. Place over filling. Fold top crust under bottom crust and crimp edges around rim to seal. Cut several slits in top crust to allow steam to escape during baking. Protect edges of crust with 2-inch-wide strip of foil. Bake according to directions in recipe for filling.

Pineapple-Rhubarb Pie

Pastry for two-crust 9-inch pie
½ cup packed brown sugar
½ cup granulated sugar
⅓ cup all-purpose flour
⅛ teaspoon ground cinnamon
1 8-ounce can pineapple
    chunks, drained
4 cups cut-up rhubarb
2 tablespoons butter or
    margarine

Stir together sugars, flour, and cinnamon. Cut pineapple chunks in half. Spread half of rhubarb in pastry-lined pan. Arrange pineapple on top. Sprinkle half of sugar mixture over fruit. Top with remaining rhubarb and sugar mixture. Dot with butter.

Adjust top crust over filling. Fold top crust under bottom crust and crimp edges around rim to seal. Cut several slits in top crust to allow steam to escape during baking. Protect edges of crust with 2-inch-wide strip of foil.

Bake in 425°F. oven 40 to 50 minutes until lightly browned and filling begins to bubble up through the slits.

Makes 8 servings

Pastry for Two-Crust 9-inch Pie

2 cups all-purpose flour
1 teaspoon salt
¾ cup shortening
Cold milk

Stir together flour and salt. Cut shortening into flour with pastry blender or two knives. Mixture should contain pieces the size of small peas.

Sprinkle milk, 1 tablespoon at a time, over flour. Toss flour mixture with a fork after each tablespoon of milk. After 4 tablespoons of milk have been used, try to gather dough together. If it doesn't hold in a ball, sprinkle another tablespoon of milk over crumbly mixture and try again. Repeat if necessary. When dough can be compressed into a ball, let it rest 10 minutes.

Divide dough in half. Roll out one portion on a lightly floured surface or pastry cloth. Make a circle 1½ inches larger than rim of a 9-inch pie pan.

Fold pastry circle into quarters and transfer to pie pan. Pat but do not stretch dough to fit pan. Add filling. Trim bottom crust to within ½ inch of rim of pie pan.

Roll out second crust the same as the first. Place over filling. Fold top crust under bottom crust and crimp edges around rim to seal. Cut several slits in top crust to allow steam to escape during baking. Protect edges of crust with 2-inch-wide strip of foil. Bake according to directions in filling recipe.

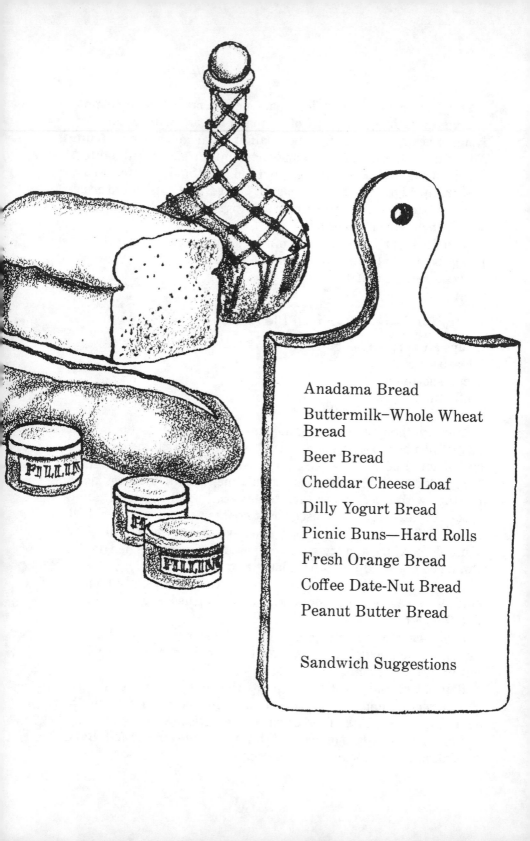

Anadama Bread

Buttermilk–Whole Wheat Bread

Beer Bread

Cheddar Cheese Loaf

Dilly Yogurt Bread

Picnic Buns—Hard Rolls

Fresh Orange Bread

Coffee Date-Nut Bread

Peanut Butter Bread

Sandwich Suggestions

6

A Loaf of Bread and . . .

Considering that bread comprises two-thirds of a sandwich, it deserves twice the attention it usually receives. Until recently it was thought of mostly as a platform for the filling. The growing popularity of mixed-grain breads and ethnic loaves or specialties has changed all this. Choosing the bread is an enjoyable part of a food shopping trip.

As good as these breads are and however much they complement a tasty filling, nothing adds pizzazz to a sandwich like homemade bread.

Both yeast and quick breads are included in this chapter. Their uses are by no means limited to sandwich making. Don't overlook buttering thin slices to serve with soups and salads.

Cold and hot sandwiches along with pointers for making and packing them for a picnic wind up the chapter.

YEAST BREADS

All of the yeast breads in this chapter are kneaded. Batter breads tend to have a more open texture and are freshest tasting soon after baking. Kneaded breads are firm textured and slice well for several days—if they last that long.

Baking yeast bread would lose its difficult-to-do image if more people approached it from a management point of view. What is seen as a long job actually is a delegation of authority. The project takes 10 minutes to mix and 10 minutes to knead the dough. From then on everything is turned over to the yeast. Being highly motivated, the yeast doesn't need supervision to do the job. At an appropriate interval you shape the loaf and let the yeast go to work again. After the second rising, the oven takes over and the job is done.

Anadama Bread

¾ cup yellow cornmeal
1 cup boiling water
½ cup molasses
1 cup milk
⅓ cup shortening
1 tablespoon salt
2 packages active dry yeast
5½ to 5¾ cups all-purpose flour
2 eggs

In small mixing bowl slowly stir cornmeal into boiling water. Blend in molasses. Set aside.

Heat milk, shortening, and salt together over low heat until shortening is almost melted. Stir slowly into cornmeal mixture. Cool to lukewarm (115–120°F.).

In large mixer bowl stir together the yeast and 3 cups of the flour. Add cornmeal mixture. Add eggs. Beat ½ minute at low speed of electric mixer, scraping sides of the bowl constantly. Beat 3 minutes at high speed, scraping the bowl as necessary.

Stir in enough of the remaining flour by hand to make dough easy to handle. Knead 10 minutes on a floured surface until smooth and elastic. Place in a greased bowl and turn dough greased side up. Cover loosely and let rise in a warm place until double in bulk, about 1 to 1½ hours.

Punch down dough. Divide in half and let rest 10 minutes. Shape into 2 loaves and place in greased 8½-by-4½-by-2½-inch loaf pans. Cover loosely and let rise until double, about 45 minutes.

Bake in 375°F. oven 30 to 40 minutes. Cover lightly with foil about 15 minutes before the end of the baking time if tops of loaves are becoming too brown. Remove from pan and cool on rack.

Makes 2 loaves

Buttermilk–Whole Wheat Bread

2 packages active dry yeast
1 cup all-purpose flour
3 to 3½ cups whole wheat flour
1 cup buttermilk
¾ cup water
⅓ cup packed brown sugar
2 tablespoons cooking oil
2 teaspoons salt

In large mixer bowl combine yeast, all-purpose flour, and 1 cup of the whole wheat flour.

Heat buttermilk, water, brown sugar, oil, and salt until just warm (120°F.) Add to yeast mixture and beat ½ minute at low speed of the electric mixer, scraping the bowl constantly. Beat 3 minutes at high speed, scraping the bowl as necessary.

Add enough of remaining whole wheat flour by hand to make dough easy to handle. Knead 10 minutes on floured board until dough is smooth and elastic. Place in a greased bowl and turn dough greased side up. Cover loosely and let rise in a warm place until double in bulk, about 1 to 1½ hours.

Punch down dough. Let rest 10 minutes. Shape into a loaf and place in greased 9-by-5-by-3-inch loaf pan. Or divide dough in half, shaping each part into a loaf and using two 8½-by-4½-by-2½-inch loaf pans. Cover loosely and let rise until double, about 45 minutes.

Bake in 375°F. oven 30 to 40 minutes for the large loaf and 25 to 35 minutes for the smaller loaves. Remove bread from pan and cool on rack.

Makes 1 large or 2 medium-sized loaves

Beer Bread

1 package active dry yeast
3½ to 4 cups all-purpose flour
1 12-ounce can beer

2 tablespoons shortening
2 tablespoons sugar
1 teaspoon salt
Melted butter

In large mixer bowl combine yeast and 2 cups of the flour.

Heat beer, shortening, sugar, and salt just until warm (120°F.), stirring occasionally. Shortening may not be completely melted. Add beer mixture to mixer bowl and beat ½ minute at low speed on electric mixer, scraping bowl constantly. Beat 3 minutes at high speed, scraping the bowl as necessary.

Add enough of the remaining flour by hand to make dough easy to handle. Knead dough 10 minutes on floured surface until smooth and elastic. Place in a greased bowl and turn dough greased side up. Cover loosely and let rise in a warm place until double in bulk, about 1 hour.

Punch down dough. Let rest 10 minutes. Shape a round loaf and place on a greased baking sheet. Cover loosely and let rise until double in bulk, about 45 minutes.

Bake in 375°F. oven 30 to 40 minutes. Cover top with foil during last 15 minutes to prevent overbrowning. Remove from sheet and cool on a rack. Brush top of loaf with melted butter while still warm.

Makes 1 loaf

Cheddar Cheese Loaf

1 package active dry yeast
3¼ to 4 cups all-purpose flour
1½ cups milk
2 tablespoons sugar
1 tablespoon cooking oil
1 teaspoon salt
1 cup shredded sharp natural
    Cheddar cheese
Melted butter

In mixer bowl combine yeast and 2 cups of the flour.

Heat milk, sugar, oil, and salt until just warm (120°F.). Add to flour mixture and beat ½ minute at low speed on electric mixer, scraping the sides of the bowl constantly. Beat 3 minutes at high speed, scraping the bowl as necessary.

Add another cup of the flour and the cheese by hand. When cheese is well distributed, add enough of the remaining flour to make the dough easy to handle.

Knead 10 minutes on floured surface until smooth and elastic. Place in greased bowl and turn greased side up. Cover loosely and let rise in a warm place until double in bulk, about 1 hour.

Punch down dough. Let rest 10 minutes. Shape into a loaf and place in greased 9-by-5-by-3-inch loaf pan. Or divide dough in half, shaping each part into a loaf, and using two 8½-by-4½-by-2½-inch loaf pans. Cover loosely and let rise until double in bulk, about 45 minutes.

Bake in 375°F. oven 30 to 35 minutes for large loaf or 25 to 30 minutes for two smaller loaves. Cover top with foil during last 15 minutes to prevent overbrowning. Remove from oven. Cool on a rack. Brush top with melted butter while still warm.

Makes 1 large loaf or 2 medium-sized loaves

Dilly Yogurt Bread

1 8-ounce carton plain yogurt
2 packages active dry yeast
¾ cup warm water
    (105–115°F.)
¼ cup shortening
3 tablespoons honey
2 teaspoons salt
½ teaspoon dried dill weed
4 to 4½ cups all-purpose flour

Let yogurt stand at room temperature while you are assembling the rest of the ingredients.

In mixer bowl dissolve yeast in warm water. Add yogurt,

shortening, honey, salt, dill weed, and 2 cups of the flour. Beat ½ minute on low speed of electric mixer, scraping the bowl constantly. Beat 3 minutes at high speed, scraping the bowl as necessary.

Add enough of the remaining flour by hand to make dough easy to handle. Knead 10 minutes on floured surface until smooth and elastic. Place in greased bowl and turn dough greased side up. Cover loosely and let rise in a warm place until double in bulk, about 45 minutes. Punch down dough.

Divide dough in half. Let rest 10 minutes. Shape each piece of dough into a loaf and place in greased 8½-by-4½-by-2½-inch loaf pans. Cover loosely and let rise until double in bulk.

Bake in 400°F. oven 30 to 35 minutes. Remove from pans. Let cool on a rack.

Makes 2 loaves

Picnic Buns

2 medium potatoes, peeled and
    sliced
1 package active dry yeast
3¼ to 3½ cups all-purpose flour
3 tablespoons butter or
    margarine
1 tablespoon sugar
1½ teaspoons salt
1 egg
Melted butter

In small saucepan cook potatoes in enough water to cover until tender. Drain, reserving liquid. Mash potatoes and set aside. Add enough water to potato liquid to make ¾ cup.

In a mixer bowl combine yeast and 1 cup of the flour.

In a saucepan heat potato liquid, butter, sugar, and salt until warm (120°F.). Add to yeast mixture and beat at low speed until smooth. Add egg and mashed potatoes and beat ½ minute at low speed, scraping the sides of the bowl constantly. Beat 3 minutes at high speed, scraping bowl as necessary.

Stir in enough of the remaining flour by hand to make a moderately stiff dough. Knead 5 minutes on a lightly floured surface. Place in a greased bowl and turn dough greased side up. Cover loosely and let rise in a warm place until nearly double, about 45 minutes. Punch down dough. Cover and let rest 10 minutes.

On a lightly floured surface divide dough in half. Cut each half into 6 pieces. Shape each piece into the shape of a hamburger bun. Place buns about 2 inches apart on greased baking sheets. Cover loosely and let rise until double in bulk, about 20 minutes. Flatten tops of buns slightly.

Bake in 350°F. oven for 18 to 20 minutes or until nicely browned. Transfer to cooling racks and brush tops with melted butter.

Makes 12 buns

Hard Rolls

2 packages active dry yeast
6¾ to 7¼ cups all-purpose flour
2½ cups water
1 tablespoon sugar
1 tablespoon cooking oil
2 teaspoons salt
Cornmeal
1 egg white
1 tablespoon water

In large mixer bowl combine yeast and 3 cups of the flour.

Heat water, sugar, oil, and salt until just warm (120°F.). Add to dry mixture. Beat ½ minute at low speed of electric mixer, scraping bowl constantly. Beat 3 minutes at high speed, scraping bowl as necessary. Stir in enough of remaining flour by hand to make dough easy to handle.

Knead 10 minutes on floured surface until dough is smooth and elastic. Place in greased bowl and turn dough greased side up. Cover loosely and let rise until double in bulk, 1 to 1½ hours. Punch down dough.

Divide dough into 18 pieces. Let rest 10 minutes. Shape each piece of dough into a rectangle 4 inches long. Place on greased, cornmeal-sprinkled baking sheets.

Make a lengthwise cut ¼ inch deep on top of each roll. Beat egg white and 1 tablespoon water just until foamy. Brush tops of rolls. Cover loosely. Let rise till double in bulk, about 1 hour.

Bake in 375°F. oven for 20 minutes. Brush again with egg white mixture. Bake 10 to 15 minutes longer or until golden brown.

Makes 18 rolls

Pita Bread (see page 12 for recipe)

QUICK BREADS

These delicious treats skip the kneading and rising steps of their yeast counterparts. However, since they slice more easily after standing for several hours, it is helpful to schedule making the loaf a day ahead of when you plan to use it.

Fresh Orange Bread

2 cups all-purpose flour
¾ cup sugar
2 teaspoons baking powder
¾ teaspoon salt
½ teaspoon baking soda
1 egg
¼ cup cooking oil
1 teaspoon grated orange peel
⅔ cup freshly squeezed orange
    juice

Stir together flour, sugar, baking powder, salt, and soda.

Beat egg well and add oil, orange peel, and orange juice. Add orange juice mixture to dry ingredients all at once, mixing only enough to moisten dry ingredients. Turn mixture into greased 8½-by-4½-by-2½-inch loaf pan. Bake in 350°F. oven 60 minutes.

Remove from pan. Cool on a rack. When cool, wrap in foil. Loaf slices better if made the day before picnic.

Makes 1 loaf

Coffee Date-Nut Bread

3 cups all-purpose flour
2½ teaspoons baking powder
½ teaspoon baking soda
8 ounces dates, cut up
½ cup chopped nuts
½ cup butter or margarine
¾ cup sugar
3 beaten eggs
1½ teaspoons vanilla
1½ cups coffee

Stir together flour, baking powder, and baking soda. Stir in dates and nuts.

Cream butter and sugar until light and fluffy. Add eggs and vanilla. Mix thoroughly.

Add flour mixture alternately with the coffee, beginning and ending with flour. Mix just until dry ingredients are moistened.

Turn mixture into 2 greased and floured 8½-by-4½-by-2½-inch loaf pans. Let stand 15 minutes.

Bake in 350°F. oven for about 40 minutes. Remove from pan. Cool on rack. Bread slices better if made the day before picnic.

Makes 2 loaves

Peanut Butter Bread

1 cup all-purpose flour
1 cup whole wheat flour

2 teaspoons baking powder
½ teaspoon baking soda
⅔ cup peanut butter
¼ cup honey
1 egg
1¼ cups milk

Stir together all-purpose flour, whole wheat flour, baking powder, and baking soda.

In mixing bowl cream peanut butter and honey. Add egg and beat well. Add dry ingredients to creamed mixture alternately with the milk. Beat just until moistened after each addition.

Turn dough into well-greased 8½-by-4½-by-2½-inch loaf pan. Bake in 350°F. oven 50 to 60 minutes. Remove from pan. Cool on rack. Wrap in foil. Bread slices better if made the day before picnic.

Makes 1 loaf

SANDWICH SUGGESTIONS

"What time do we eat?" holds the same importance for sandwiches as other picnic foods. It's OK to brown-bag sandwiches when eating time is no more than 3 hours away from the refrigerator. Most fillings need help keeping cold beyond that length of time.

Frozen sandwiches in an insulated lunch box will be thawed by mealtime. Lettuce, if used, wilts fast unless carried in a cooler. Cold mayonnaise mixtures for one or two sandwiches are satisfactory in a chilled vacuum jar. When quantity of filling increases, it's best to carry chilled mayonnaise and ingredients separately and combine just before spreading and eating the sandwich.

Lunch Box Sandwiches

1. Sliced Muenster Cheese and Red Currant Jelly on buttered, thin-sliced white sandwich bread.

2. Peanut Butter with sliced Pimiento-stuffed Olives on white or whole wheat bread.

3. Sardines with Bermuda Onion Rings on buttered dark rye bread.

   Picnic pointer: Carry sardines in unopened can along with unsliced onion. Pack a small knife for slicing onion and assemble sandwiches on the spot.

4. Cold Roast Pork, Pickled Beet Slices, and Cucumber on buttered light rye bread.

   Picnic pointer: Freeze pork sandwich. Carry beet slices and small unpeeled cucumber to picnic in chilled wide-mouth bottle. At serving time slice cucumber and add pickled beets and cucumber to thawed sandwich.

5. Cold sliced Tongue with Colby or Brick Cheese on buttered pumpernickel bread.

   Picnic pointer: Cook beef tongue the day before planned use. Simmer 3 to 4 hours, covered with boiling salted water to which a small sliced onion and a few peppercorns are added. Let the tongue cool in cooking liquid 1 hour before refrigerating it. When thoroughly chilled, remove skin from tongue and slice. Freeze sandwich or carry sliced tongue in insulated cooler.

6. Open-faced Salami and Italian Salad on buttered thin-sliced rye bread.

   Picnic pointer: Top salami with 2 or 3 tablespoons Italian salad (diced cooked carrots, finely cut cooked green beans, small cooked peas, and mayonnaise). Combine all ingredients for salad and chill. Carry in chilled wide-mouth vacuum bottle.

7. Cold Roast Beef with Hot Mustard and Gherkins on buttered kaiser roll.

   Picnic pointer: Transfer a small amount of mustard (horseradish, English, Dijon, or other choice from gourmet shelf) to a small disposable container so that you do not have to carry the whole jar of mustard to and from the picnic. Freeze sandwich. At serving time slather on the mustard and add gherkins to sandwich.

8. Blue Cheese–sliced Egg–sliced Radish on split and buttered hard roll.

    Picnic pointer: Keep all ingredients cold. Shell and slice hard-cooked egg at serving time. Carry mayonnaise in chilled wide-mouth vacuum bottle.

9. Sliced Turkey with Jellied Cranberry Sauce on white or whole wheat sandwich bread.

    Picnic pointer: Freeze turkey sandwich. Pack portion-sized slice of canned cranberry sauce in plastic sandwich bag. Complete sandwich when ready to eat.

10. Bacon with Liver Sausage on split and buttered rye rolls.

    Picnic pointer: Blend crisp-cooked crumbled bacon with softened liver sausage. Chill and pack in chilled wide-mouth vacuum jar.

Hot Sandwiches

1. Italian Sausage and Peppers on split and buttered chunks of Italian bread.

    Picnic pointer: Shape Italian sausage into tiny meat balls and cook thoroughly. Cook julienne strips of green pepper and onion rings in a small amount of olive oil until tender. Spoon hot sausage and vegetables into heated wide-mouth vacuum bottle.

2. Barbecues in a Hollow Bun.

    Picnic pointer: Heat your favorite barbecue beef or Sloppy Joe mixture and spoon into heated wide-mouth vacuum bottle. Cut a plug about 1 inch in diameter from the center of an unsliced sandwich bun, making sure it does not go clear through the bottom. Set aside plug. (It will be lid for sandwich.) Using your index finger, hollow out a space in the center of the bun. Add some of the bread crumbs that accumulate to the barbecue mixture to thicken it slightly. At serving time spoon hot barbecue mixture into hollow and top with plug lid.

Recipe Index